D0378518

# TRAITOR

BY

## DANIEL MASSIEH

OPEN THE GATES PUBLISHING

SAN DIEGO, CALIFORNIA

# TRAITOR
By Daniel Massieh

© 2009 OTG Publishing
Published by Open The Gates Publishing
PO Box 270333 San Diego, California 92198

www.openthegates.org

ISBN-13: 978-0-615-30807-4
ISBN-10: 0615308074

All scripture quotations, unless otherwise indicated, are taken from the New King James Version®. Copyright © 1982 by Thomas Nelson, Inc. Used by permission. All rights reserved.

All Rights Reserved
No part of this publication may be reproduced, stored in a retrieval system, or transmitted in any form or by any means - electronic, mechanical, photocopy, recording, or otherwise - without the prior express written consent of OTG Publishing, with the exception of brief excerpts in magazine articles and/or reviews.

Printed in the United States of America

To my wonderful wife, Samia,
and our five precious children,
Joshua, Heidi, Christine, Ashley & Johnny.
You all have been my treasure
and have helped greatly during our thirty
years on the mission field.

# Acknowledgements

When it comes to acknowledgments, my Lord and Savior Jesus Christ must come first. I can do nothing without Him. The thirty years I've been a born again Christian have been a great adventure. I am blessed. I was saved in 1979 in my homeland of Egypt, but for the past twenty-five years I have been in the United States. My heart goes out to people who don't know the saving grace of Jesus Christ. That is the purpose of this book – to show them the truth.

There are many individuals who helped make this book possible and I wish to thank them from the bottom of my heart and say this with the love of Christ.

My deep appreciation to Pastor Ray Bentley, my pastor, and Maranatha Chapel for their endless support of my ministry.

To Merrill Nanigian whom God sent my way for such a time as this. Her commitment and sacrifice in translating the manuscripts and editing this book is amazing. It's more than I can comprehend! She spent tremendous amounts of hours, days, and months to make this book available.

My thanks to the Open the Gates team at Maranatha Chapel, and the Board of Directors, my greatest source of strength and inspiration.

I praise the Lord for Ben and Marie Barnhart, a really sweet couple, who encouraged me to publish the book and made it easy for me to move forward. I'm thankful for their creativity with the cover and layout of the manuscripts.

My thanks to Rick Monroe of Good News, etc. newspaper, who also spent many hours in editing the final copy before publishing.

A special thanks to Pastor Latif, who discipled me in Egypt. To all Christian believers in Egypt who stood beside me during the early years of my faith, and have supported me and hosted me in their homes for days and months.

Thank you to all the pastors who allowed me to stand in their pulpits to preach and share what God has done in my life.

I also appreciate all the friends and prayer warriors who are praying for me, my family and this ministry.

To all my beloved friends who have partnered with me in this ministry. I appreciate all of the skills our heavenly Father has given to you and how willing you are to use them for His glory. May God bless all of you. I pray that God will reward you in every way with His goodness and grace. He is the King of all the ages, who never fades away. Glory be to Him alone, our wise God, forever and ever.

# Table of Contents

# *Introduction*

I met brother Daniel Massieh as a guest on my TV program, *Daring Question*, in September 2007. I was touched greatly by his testimony. I listened intently to the ways God has and is miraculously working in his life. I am blessed by his humble nature and the strong love he displays for his brothers and sisters of Islamic decent. He is bold for the sake of the gospel, spreading the good news at every opportunity. Even through the challenges of life that we all face, he stays focused, using his time, effort and finances to serve the Lord by helping others to know the truth. It is an honor to know him.

Seeing the ways that brother Daniel has experienced the love of God, which includes the modern day miracle of his son being raised from the dead, I am truly inspired. Brother Daniel's testimony is a good reminder for us all that, Jesus is alive yesterday, today, and forever! The same Jesus that raised the dead two thousand years ago is still raising flesh and spirit today!

I pray that one of your goals while reading this book will be to draw closer to God, your Creator. Please listen to His voice through the words that follow. Life teaches us that we can all learn through the experiences of others. I pray that through reading this, whether you are Muslim or Christian, you will be enriched in your understanding, education and spiritual development. I gratefully pray that the Master and Creator of the universe will change your life dramatically as you read these pages. May He make you a blessing just as He made brother Daniel a blessing, for the sake of His glory.

Rashid, the Moroccan

Host of *Daring Question*

As a young man in his early twenties, Daniel lived a normal life in the city of Cairo. He was like many of the Egyptian youths of his age. He believed that Christianity was a religion of immorality. He believed that all Westerners were Christians. He did not know the truth about genuine Christianity. When he became aware of the reality of Christ's holiness, love, and momentous sacrifice, he could no longer stand silent. He became a witness, sharing the love of Christ to many of his kinsmen. He faced hardship and imprisonment because of his testimony for Christ. You will learn in this book how God delivered him from all sorts of calamity. I pray that this book will be a blessing to many, encouraging them also to be servants and witnesses for Christ.

Father Zakaria Butrous

# Forward

"Now there was a man of the Pharisees named Nicodemus, a member of the Jewish ruling council. He came to Jesus at night and said, 'Rabbi, we know you are a teacher who has come from God. For no one could perform the miraculous signs you are doing if God were not with him.'

In reply, Jesus declared, 'I tell you the truth; no one can see the kingdom of God unless he is born again.'

'How can a man be born again when he is old,' Nicodemus asked. 'Surely he cannot enter a second time into his mother's womb to be born!'

Jesus answered, 'I tell you the truth, no one can enter the kingdom of God unless he is born of water and the Spirit. Flesh gives birth to flesh, but the Spirit gives birth to the Spirit.'"

John 3:1-6

Dear Reader,

1.) Do you know what it means to be born again from the Spirit?

2.) Do know the difference between one who has been born according to the flesh and one who has been born according to the Spirit?

3.) Do you want to be born from above, that is, to be born from the Spirit and alive to God?

In this book my friend, Daniel Massieh has given us his story. He has told us how he became born again from above. I was an eyewitness to everything he has written in this book. I advise you to have a Bible with you as you read his story and to look up the references that brother Daniel shares. If God tugs on your heart and moves you as you read these pages, please ask Him earnestly to show you who He is. Humbly tell Him that you would like to be born again of the Spirit. May you join the millions of others who know their Creator so that you will shine brightly with His love until the whole world is filled with His glory. To Him be the glory forever and ever!

Your servant,

Pastor Latif Fahim Morcous

# A NOTE FROM THE AUTHOR

Throughout the book, I will be referencing the Bible, the Qur'an and the Hadith. Muslims believe in the Hadith which records the traditions of Muhammad's words and actions

The traditions of Muhammad are the practical interpretations of the Qur'an. The role of Muhammad was to convey the Qur'an as he received it, to interpret it, and to practice it fully. His interpretations and practices produced what is known as the traditions of Muhammad and these interpretations are called the Hadith.

The Hadith comprises traditional accounts of the things said or done by Muhammad and his companions. Men such as Al-Bukhari recorded Muhammad's words and actions in the Hadith. It is used to shed light on the teachings of the Qur'an analogous to the manner in which the Talmud expands on the Jewish writings of the Torah. The Hadith is a set of parallel books to the Qur'an and serves as a supplement to the Qur'an. Each Hadith is a saying or comment attributed to Muhammad and a chain of comments documenting how the report was transmitted. The Sunni and Shia branches of Islam have differing Hadiths because of the different paths of succession from Islam.

The Most recognized collection of the Hadith is the collection of Shih Al-Bukhari (194—256 H). He spent sixteen years compiling his research, and ended up with 3,295 Hadiths divided into 97 "books" with 3,450 chapters. Each Hadith was checked for compatibility with the Qur'an. Shih Muslim is a much larger collection. Abul Husain was a student of Bukhari. He collected three hundred thousand Hadiths. Twelve thousand were accepted by Bukhari. Muslims scholars consider the collection of Bukhari and Shih Muslim to be the most authentic books after the Qur'an. Two partial collections have a smaller following in Islamic academia. There are other partial collection of Sunan Abu Dawuud and Malik'I Muwatta that are about one half the size of those by Bukhari and Muslim, but they influence such Islamic sects as the Druze.

*"He it is Who shapes you in the wombs as He pleases. There is no god but He, the Exalted in Might, the Wise."*

*Qur'an 3:6*

# Preface

Dear reader, the following is the story of my spiritual journey. It has not been an easy trek for me, but one that I feel I need to share with you, especially those of you who are my blood brothers, the decedents of Ishmael.

My story takes many twists and turns and may seem a little disjointed, but if you stay with me you will come to a rich treasure. So let me begin here, by telling you my background.

I was born into a Muslim family. Both of my parents were Muslim. My father's family originally came from Turkey. My father was born and raised in our beloved Egypt. He met my mother at Cairo University where they were both students. Together they raised three children.

After they married, my father was hired as a manager for a large travel firm in Giza, a well known city in Egypt. The firm specialized in helping Muslim clients make the hajj (pilgrimage) to

Mecca in Saudi Arabia. My father was very active and influential in the community. Because of his connections he was able to obtain visas for thousands of Muslims who desired to make the hajj.

My parents were very loving people and raised me in a caring family atmosphere. We learned that as a family it was important to love each other and stay united. We were taught to respect other people and to be good Muslims.

My father labored hard to instill in us the importance of being a good Muslim. I learned to follow all the tenants of Islam and read the Qur'an daily. Five times a day he would roll out his prayer rug and pray to Allah. When I was six years old he taught me to pray. I can remember going with him and my brother to pray every Friday at the mosque. We would stand with the other worshippers in a straight line according to the Sunnah of the prophet Muhammad, so that our prayers would be acceptable to Allah. We would all shout, "Allah Akbar!" while bowing our foreheads to the ground.

I remember one day asking my father why some of the worshippers at the mosque had a dark spot in the middle of their foreheads. He told me that this was a sign of great piety. These men were so devout in their prayers that they would pray more than the required five times a day. Each time they prayed, their foreheads would touch the ground. Eventually their foreheads formed a dark spot, showing their devotion and submission to Allah. He added that in heaven these men would be granted a higher degree of reward than the average Muslim who only did the required five daily prayers.

The example of these men so impressed me that I was determined to be like them and have a dot on my forehead. I began to pray daily, more than the five required times. I did this for many months. When I did not see the dot appear, I became disappointed and stopped doing the extra prayers. Later I learned that these devout men had a little rock they would place on the ground. When they bowed low during prayer, their foreheads would hit the rock and eventually a scar formed. With time, the scar got darker and darker.

When the box of the Zakat (alms) was passed during Friday prayers at the mosque, my father would give us money to donate. According to the Qur'an, each Muslim was to give 2.5% of his monthly income to the mosque. At the end of this prayer time, we would repeat after the Imam a curse over the enemies of Islam. The curse went something like this, **"Allahumma, destroy our enemies, kill them, may their wives be widows, may their children be orphans, destroy their homes and make them homeless. Allahumma, give the Muslims victory over their enemies, Allahumma, give us blessings, one after another."** After each curse the congregation would agree by saying "amen."

As a young man I was considered gifted with a bright future ahead of me. I had committed many chapters from the Qur'an to memory. When I reached high school age, I began to struggle with temptations. This made me even more devoted to Islam and I would pray fervently for Allah to save me from sin.

Every year my family fasted during Ramadan. Two of my fondest childhood memories were celebrating the holidays of Eid-ul-Fitr and Eid-ul-Adha. My father would buy each of us new clothes and shoes for these occasions and we would proudly go to the mosque and sit among the worshippers. Eid-ul-Fitr is the first day after Ramadan where we break the fast. We would joyfully exchange gifts and share cookies and sweets with our neighbors and friends.

Eid-ul-Adha is the holiday where we remember Abraham's willingness to sacrifice his son. The story tells how Abraham's son was spared when a ram was sent to redeem him instead. I loved to sing the traditional song of Eid-ul-Adha which goes like this, **"Labbaik Allahumma Labbaik, Labbaik La sharika laka Labbaik en el hammadah Laka wa el neemata laka La sharik Laka Labbaik…"** It means, "Lord we are answering your call, there is no other God beside Allah. For to you belongs all thanksgiving and grace. There is no other God besides you." All Muslims around the world knew this song. After our time at the mosque, we would return home to a great feast that my mother had prepared, which included a lamb to represent the ram in the story of Abraham and his son.

My mother was a very sweet, lovely lady. She was born in a prominent Egyptian family. Her father was one of the wealthiest men in Egypt. He was a famous mayor who was given the title Basha (mayor). His full name was Mostafa Khiret Basha and there is a well known street in Cairo that is named after him.

My mother was well educated as a lawyer. She was also fluent in French. Her favorite occupation, however, was being a mother to her three children, and she stayed home to raise us. She was a very devoted mother. She would watch over our studies and was always present to help us with our homework. She made us wonderful meals and made sure that we had proper nutrition. When we grew older and would go out for the evening. She would not sleep until we arrived home safely.

I remember one time when I was a teenager. I had gone to Alexandria with some of my friends. Alexandria was a two to three hour drive from our home in Cairo. On our second day in Alexandria, we heard a knock on the door. Who was it? It was my mother with a gallon of milk in her arms! When I asked her why she had come all this way, she said that she wanted to make sure that I wouldn't forget to drink my milk! My friends and I still laugh when we remember this story.

I thank God for the wonderful family that God gave to me. Now, let me tell you the rest of my story.

*Doqy City, Cairo, Egypt,*
*December 19, 1981*

# 1

# Should Such a Man as I Flee?

Our gathering at the apartment in Doqy was interrupted by the sound of the doorbell. Hani and I looked curiously at each other. I thought that perhaps this was the taxi driver I had invited earlier. Hani quickly rose to see who was at the door. There were two tall men dressed in suits. Hani did not recognize the two men and was quite sure they had never met with our group before.

"Is Mohammed Kamel here?" they asked.

"Who are you and why do you want to speak with Mohammed?" Hani replied.

They identified themselves as secret police, showed their badges, and stated again that they wanted to speak with me. My friend came back inside the apartment with a wry smile on his face.

"Mohammed, what did you do today?" he asked. "Did you do anything wrong?"

"What do you mean?" I replied.

"Two secret policemen are at the door asking for you." Then he whispered, "You can slip out through the kitchen door to the fire escape."

I was surprised at Hani's suggestion. Should such a man as I flee? I told Hani, "I am not afraid of the police. I will go talk with them." The two men were waiting for me at the gate.

"I am Mohammed," I said.

They introduced themselves to me by name while presenting their badges. One of men, Mr. Alaa, said, "Mr. Kamal, we need you to come with us down to our headquarters. We need to ask you some questions. It shouldn't take more than a half hour and then you can return home." I believed them and went willingly.

As we descended the elevator from the twelfth floor apartment, there was silence. We exited the building to find a Mercedes waiting for us. We climbed in. Mr. Alaa sat in the front, next to the driver. The other man sat next to me in the back as a guard, I assumed. No one spoke until I broke the silence.

"What questions would you like me to answer?"

"We just have some routine questions to ask, and then you will be free to return home," replied Mr. Alaa.

Despite his nonchalant manner, I wasn't convinced. This wasn't my first encounter with the secret police. The first one had occurred a few months earlier and I was detained for a few hours. This time, however, I sensed something different. I had an uneasy feeling. Oddly enough, at twenty-three years of age, I was not afraid of what may lie ahead. As I sat in the Mercedes, I was filled with a great sense of peace like there was an unusual Strength upholding me.

After a fifteen-minute drive, the Mercedes turned into a long driveway pulling up to an enormous security gate. One of the secret police raised his hand to identify himself to the guards. The gate opened and the car proceeded. I realized that we were entering the headquarters where the highest officers of the Egyptian Secret

Service conducted their business. This would be the equivalent to the highest offices of the American FBI. It was close to eight o'clock at night when Mr. Alaa began to question me. He asked about my family and friends. He asked me about a conversation that took place in a taxi earlier that day. He questioned me about the meeting at the apartment in Doqy and why I was there. I answered all of his questions honestly.

*"...teaching the things which concern the Lord Jesus Christ with all confidence, no one forbidding him."*

*Acts 28:31*

# 2

# Egyptian Secret Service

Mr. Alaa asked me to tell him my story. He wanted to know what compelled me to witness publicly for Christ and why I left Islam and converted to Christianity. I started by telling Mr. Alaa about my background and the prominent Muslim family I was from. My father was a wealthy businessman and my mother was a lawyer. My uncle was a general in the Egyptian army and my brother was a judge in the military. My cousin's husband was the chief of the police academy and I had another cousin who had been an assistant to Hosni Mubarak while he was a cabinet member to Anwar Sadat. I was very proud of my Egyptian roots. I explained that my parents named me Mohammed Kamel because I was born the same day as the Prophet Muhammad.

I told Mr. Alaa that I had been an enemy of the Christians. I believed them to be infidels who believed in three gods. I believed that the Bible was an unclean book which encouraged adultery, drinking, and obscene acts. I thought that the communion celebration was an opportunity for Christians to get drunk and have orgies. Like most Muslims, I believed that the behavior seen in American and European movies and in the media was representative of Christianity. I believed that if I were to attend a church service I would see with my own eyes these shameful acts being committed by the Christians.

I told Mr. Alaa that my conversion began with a desire to find out what Christians do at their places of worship. I wanted to witness their evil acts so that I could share this with my Muslim friends. I told him that I never intended to become a Christian at all. I wanted nothing more than to prove their beliefs absurd and sinful. I thought if I were to go to a church service I would see the parishioners engaging in wild dancing and sexual sin. I thought I would see people drinking liquor from the communion cup and getting drunk. So I began this quest by asking my friend Mamdouh to take me to a church service.

Mamdouh was a nominal Christian and he attended the Orthodox Church. We had been friends since middle school. I told Mamdouh that I wanted to learn about Christianity, although I really had no intention to do so. I only wanted to get access to the church so that I could witness their sinful acts. Mamdouh was suspicious of my intentions. Not wanting to bring harm to his church, he decided instead to take me to the Evangelical church in his neighborhood.

It was a Friday evening in May, 1979, when we arrived at the Evangelical church in Tahrer Square in Cairo. This was the first time I set foot in a church. On the front of the building was a big clock tower. It was seven o'clock. We took the stairs to the second floor and entered the meeting room where there were many people sitting in chairs facing the preacher. I asked Mamdouh if I needed to take my shoes off as is the custom before entering the mosque. He responded, "No, Hamada, we are not going to the mosque." Mamdouh was a very funny guy and his nickname for me was "Hamada," which means "cool dude."

We took a seat in the back of the room. I was glad because I did not want to draw attention to myself. I had never seen so many Christians in one place. They were all sitting on chairs and not on the ground like in the mosques. I was looking at their faces and I wondered if they would notice that I was a Muslim and not one of them.

The preacher at the front of the church caught my attention. He was speaking about the devil. He was saying how the devil can appear as an angel of light to deceive people. He was very funny and the people were laughing as they listened to him. I was wondering if the people noticed me. I felt very self conscious. Did they know that a Muslim man was attending their service?

After a few minutes the preacher asked the group to pray. I elbowed my friend and asked him, "What do I do?" He told me just to close my eyes and talk to God. I thought to myself, "Ah ha! He wants me to close my eyes so that I will not see the bad things that they are about to do!" I believed that this was when the Christians would start behaving badly. Now was my chance to catch them! I kept my eyes open hoping to see these acts being committed. But to my disappointment I only saw the people with bowed heads praying. I thought that Mamdouh had alerted them that I was coming to their service so that I wouldn't be able to witness them doing the bad things. I thought to myself, "I will come again to the church, unannounced. Perhaps the next time I will see the bad things happening."

Towards the end of the church meeting, the preacher asked one of the parishioners to pray. The man stood up and started to pray out loud. I thought that he was reciting a memorized prayer, like we do in Islam. I thought that if I came to the church the next time I would need to know this prayer in case the preacher called on me to pray out loud. I was determined to be prepared for my next visit to the church so that I wouldn't look like an outsider. I asked my friend Mamdouh to write down a Christian prayer for me so that I could take it and memorize it. He took out a piece of paper and wrote out "The Lord's Prayer" (See Matthew 6:9). He told me this is a prayer all Christians know.

We returned to Mamdouh's home where I was spending the night. I went to his room and sat on the bed to memorize the prayer. I read over the prayer. It started with the words, **"Our Father in heaven."**

The first two words grabbed me! I thought, "Our Father? How can God be a father?" Muslims would never dare to call Allah, "Father" or "Dad." As Muslims, we are taught that Allah is our master, but never a father! Allah is far away from us, we can never approach him or come near to him. Yet, the Christians have the audacity to call God "Daddy!" I thought, "How ridiculous and disrespectful for Christians to address God this way! Do these Christians really believe that God is actually their father? This was certainly blasphemy."

I was blown away by the pathetic beliefs of these Christians! I casually opened the window, looked out, and mockingly asked, "God, did you marry my mother? Are you my father?"

Then, very suddenly and unexpectedly, I felt an overwhelming Presence enter the room. It was a strong comforting presence that I could feel to the very core of my inner soul. It was telling me, *"Yes, I AM your Father."* I was completely surrounded by God's presence! I was enveloped by an indescribable love, God's love *for me, a fatherly* love, in a way that I had never experienced before. God was announcing to me at that very moment that He was my heavenly Father!

I felt like a little child that had been estranged from his daddy for twenty-three years and now had been found. This love was so strong that I wanted to proclaim it to everyone, "God is my Father! God, the Creator of everything, is my Father! God Most Powerful is my Father! The Lord of all lords is *my Father!"*

All night long, I felt myself hugging God and He was hugging me. God's Spirit began reminding me of all the things I did wrong. I began confessing every sin to Him. I told Him that I was so sorry for entering the church as a deceiver, for misleading the Christian people into thinking I was interested in becoming a Christian.

Becoming aware of my sins and how they grieved the Father made me cry in a horrible way. I cried so hard that my friend, Mamdouh, heard me from his room. When he found out why I was crying he couldn't believe that this prayer, The Lord's Prayer, could make me cry like this.

That night I slept very deeply. When I awoke the next morning I felt like I had shed a heavy camel that was riding on my shoulders. Peace and comfort filled my heart. I learned later that this is what the Bible means when it says, **"Therefore if the Son makes you free, you shall be free indeed"** (John 8:36). This was the happiest day of my life, when God lightened my load with His amazing love and grace.

*"...I believed and therefore I spoke."*

*2 Corinthians 4:13*

# 3

# Unashamed

After I became a believer I had a burning in my heart to share with others the truth that Christ was the Savior of mankind. I was weary of holding back and in fact, I could not. The love of God was manifested so strongly to me that I had to tell Muslims and others of the wonderful news that Jesus died for their sins too. Therefore, I purposed in my heart to take the gospel to all of my Muslim friends and relatives, even strangers. I would take the gospel everywhere I went. I shared with people in the market place, in the bus station and in taxis. I felt exactly like Paul the apostle when he said, "**...I believed and therefore I spoke...**" (2 Corinthians 4:13).

I realized that **every soul is precious** to God and is in need of knowing the message of His love. I decided I would not waste the precious moments I was given on this earth. I was determined to tell people wherever I went about Jesus. This desire pushed me to walk through the crowded bus stations of Egypt and cry out with a loud voice, "Have you heard about Jesus Christ?"

Instead of saying good morning to my friends I would ask them, "Have you heard about Jesus Christ? Have you read what it says about Him in the Bible?" Everyone who knew me was shocked by my words because they knew my Muslim background. I used every opportunity to share the salvation of Christ with my Muslim friends, even those who I knew when I attended Cairo University.

Publicly proclaiming Christ is a dangerous task in a country where Islam is the official religion, especially if you were born a Muslim. Our law is subject to the demands and teaching of Islam which forbids anyone from sharing Christ with Muslims. In fact, the law of Islam demands that such a person be killed. But these laws did not in any way hinder me from sharing the good news about the love of Christ. God gave me supernatural boldness and I was not concerned with what man would do to me (See Hebrews 13:6). I felt as the apostle Paul, "...woe is me if I do not preach the gospel!" (1 Corinthians 9:16).

I would intentionally go inside a high building and go up and down the elevator to share with people. The higher the building, the more time I would have a captive audience. I would repeat this many times a day, until I felt that I had shared with at least ten new people. If at the end of the day I had not reached ten new people with the news that Jesus was their Savior I would get into a taxi and share with the taxi driver about Jesus. I would not go to sleep until I knew I had accomplished my goal.

When I knew that I had met my quota of sharing Christ's love and the good news of the gospel I would be filled with joy. As it is written, "I am a debtor both to Greeks and to barbarians, both to wise and to unwise. So, as much as is in me, I am ready to preach the gospel to you who are in Rome also" (Romans 1:14-15). I was a debtor to Muslims and I was ready to take the gospel to them anywhere possible.

## FROM MOHAMMED TO DANIEL

In one of the Bible studies that I attended after I became a Christian I learned about the prophet Daniel. The Scripture says of him, **"But Daniel purposed in his heart that he would not defile himself with the portion of the king's delicacies, nor with the wine which he drank; therefore he requested of the chief of the eunuchs that he might not defile himself"** (Daniel 1:8). After hearing this, I fell in love with this character, Daniel. I was amazed how he insisted on worshipping his God, standing firm even in the face of a gruesome death.

In one story, Daniel was thrown into a Lion's Den because he refused to pray to the king of Babylon. God miraculously saved him from the mouth of the hungry lions (See Daniel 6). My heart burned within me as I read and reflected on this story, and I determined to change my given name. I told all my friends and family no longer to call me by the name "Mohammed Kamel" but instead to call me by the name "Daniel Abdel Massieh." Which means Daniel the servant of the Messiah. I was honored to carry this new title because, like Daniel, I had purposed in my heart to follow the one true God.

I vowed that I would never again follow Islam, but that I would follow my Savior, Jesus, until the very end. Like Daniel in the Bible, I was willing to suffer for the name of Jesus even if this meant prison or death. I was unaware at this time of what in store for me. I refused to defile myself, **"that they might obtain a better resurrection"** (Hebrews 11:35).

## WHY ARE CHRISTIANS ASHAMED?

I was always asking myself the question, "Why are Christians in Egypt ashamed to share the gospel with Muslims?" I would see Muslims freely spreading the Qur'an in all of Egypt. They would boldly give out the Qur'an in buses and many public places. Yet, I never witnessed one Christian giving out Christian literature or proclaiming the gospel publicly. These Christians should know that the gospel is the power of salvation to all who believe. Just as the apostle Paul declared, **"For I am not ashamed of the gospel of Christ, for it is** the power of God to salvation for everyone who believes..." (Romans 1:16).

The conviction that Jesus is indeed the way, the truth and the life (John 14:6) was a fire within me. I convinced my pastor to give me New Testaments so that I could pass them out to Muslims. He was concerned that I would be harmed or killed. I insisted that he let me pass them out and he finally gave me almost one hundred New Testaments.

I took that stack of New Testaments with joy and gladness and promptly went to the crowded Cairo Bus Station. I strategically handed out the New Testaments to those heading for Alexandria. I figured that since the ride from Cairo to Alexandria is two or more hours this would provide them with the perfect reading material! I went through the back door of the bus and placed a New Testament on each person's lap. There was not one passenger that did not receive a New Testament. I felt no fear at all as I was passing out the Bibles. Instead I felt great joy for the honor of spreading the good news.

Just as I was leaving the bus one of the passengers grabbed my hand and with a smile on his face asked me, "What are you doing?" I sensed in my spirit that he was a Christian. I proudly responded to him that I was giving the passengers a copy of the New Testament. He nodded and shook my hand gratefully.

I was full of joy knowing that I was fulfilling Jesus' command to His disciples, **"Go therefore and make disciples of all the nations..."** (Matthew 28:19). This verse tells us that the entire world needs to hear the gospel which means, "good news." After Jesus gave this command His disciples went out to complete it. They traveled everywhere, far and near, to spread the good news. As it is written, **"And they went out and preached everywhere, the Lord working with them and confirming the word through the accompanying signs"** (Mark 16:20).

Christians must obey Christ's command to go to all the nations, including the Muslim nations, to bring the good news. I am amazed by the Christians that say they love Christ yet they do not obey His commandment. They remain silent while the world starves for His salvation and His love. Jesus said, **"If you love Me, keep My commandments"** (John 14:15).

*"And other sheep I have which are not of this fold;
them also I must bring, and they will hear My voice;
and there will be one flock and one shepherd."*

*John 10:16*

# 4

# Michael and Zaynab

I was invited to speak at a church meeting in Cairo. While I was waiting at the bus station, I saw a young couple in their mid-twenties. I noticed that the man had a cross around his neck and something inside me urged me to speak with the couple. I approached them and introduced myself to them as Daniel. The young man shook my hand and told me that his name was Michael. I was surprised when the young lady introduced herself as Zaynab. When I heard her name I was happy because I thought she was a Muslim convert like me. I found out, however, that she was a Muslim who was dating a nominal Christian man.

My bus was running late so I took the opportunity to witness to them. I started by asking Michael which church he was attending.

"I do not attend any church," he replied. "Zeze is a Muslim," he said, affectionately referring to his girlfriend.

I thought this was very strange because in Egypt it is very

rare to see a Christian man dating a Muslim woman. The culture would never allow them to get married unless one of them converted to the other's religion. I was not sure what was happing between both of them, but my feeling was that something was wrong.

"Have you heard about Jesus?" I asked Zeze. "Have you read the Bible before?"

"No, I am a Muslim," she said.

When she said this I took the opportunity to tell her my testimony. I told her how I was born Muslim and became a Christian. Michael and Zeze were shocked when I said this. They were wide eyed and had bewildered looks on their faces. They said they had never heard such a thing.

Michael especially was looking at me very intently. He couldn't believe what I was saying about my background. Both of our busses were very late which allowed me enough time to witness to them.

I asked the couple, "Where are you heading?"

Michael said, "I am waiting for Zeze's bus to come." As we were talking, the bus came, she got on and said goodbye. Then Michael said, "I would love if you could come to my home. I want to hear your whole story."

"I am on my way to church. If you come with me to church I would be happy to come to your home after," I said.

We went together to church then returned to his home and he shared his story with me. He told me, "ZeZe and I have been dating for many years and we love each other, but we cannot get married. ZeZe's parents are strict Muslims, and her father works for the secret police. They are putting a lot of pressure on her to adhere to the Sharia code and she is afraid of them."

Michael continued, "Her family would only allow her to marry me if I agreed to convert to Islam. I love her so much that I agreed so we could be married. We have set an appointment to go to the mosque to announce my intention to convert to Islam."

It was very surprising for me to learn that the appointment

was to take place the very next day! I knew then that the Holy Spirit had certainly intended for me to share with him and that it wasn't an accident that I met them at the bus station.

When he shared with me his story I felt great sorrow and grief in my heart. I could see how Satan was working hard to destroy Michael's life through his relationship with ZeZe. It was very sad to see how easily nominal Christians brush aside their heritage, not even considering the Christ who died for them. In their haste to satisfy their desires, they will renounce the eternal Lover of their souls.

I shared my whole story with Michael. I told him how I first encountered God's love for me through The Lord's Prayer. I told him how He changed my life, freeing me from the bondage of sin, and moved me from darkness to the light of Christ. I assured him that God's love for him is very great, and that it was not an accident that I met him and ZeZe at the bus station that day.

In all the times that I had used this bus line this was the very first time that my bus did not show up. I realized that it was God orchestrating the circumstance, so that I could meet Michael and ZeZe and that Michael would be rescued from carrying out his agreement to convert to Islam.

I asked Michael, "Why do you think we met at the bus station this afternoon?" I answered the question for him, saying, "It is because I was a Muslim who became a Christian. The Lord knew that my testimony would help you see the truth about Islam and Christianity. Also, The Lord wanted you to see that Muslims are becoming Christians. God wants to rescue you from Satan's clutches. It is Satan's desire to entrap you in the false religion of Islam and destroy your life."

I shared with Michael that Christ died for him on the cross. I gave him many examples in my own life of Christ's changing power. I explained to him that he should not be converting to Islam, but rather he should fully surrender himself to the God of his heritage and then help Muslims to convert to Christianity.

I encouraged him not to be afraid of ZeZe's father or her

family. I shared with him the persecution I received from my own family after I became a Christian and how I stood firm believing that they would someday come to know Christ as their Savior as well. I encouraged him to receive Christ and then stand for Him and not fear what might happen.

I asked him this question, "Michael, if you died today, where would your soul go?"

"I do not know," he answered.

"And what will happen if you go through with this conversion to Islam just to marry ZeZe? You might have some temporary pleasure but upon your death, you will perish in hell."

I quoted many verses for Michael from the Bible to support my words. After awhile he began to cry. I could see that the Holy Spirit was touching his heart, so I asked him, "Are you willing to accept Christ?"

"Yes," he said and prayed with me a prayer asking Jesus to come into his heart. He also asked the Lord to forgive him for renouncing Jesus in front of ZeZe. His prayer was mixed with his tears and I couldn't clearly hear what he was saying to God, but I knew by the Spirit that he had truly repented and accepted Christ into his heart.

After he prayed, a big smile formed on his face. The joy of forgiveness was shining on his face. I could see the love, joy and peace of Christ in his eyes and flooding his heart. He gave me a big hug thanking me for sharing the truth with him and how Christ changed my life. Now he too could see how God had been working to save him by sending me to meet him in the bus station that afternoon.

I found out that he worked in a hair salon. He was so grateful that God sent me to him that he offered me a whole lifetime of free haircuts at his salon! From that time on he was my personal barber and I never had to pay for another haircut while I was in Egypt. He was always sharp and professional and I always got the best haircuts. I was very happy that he had come to know his eternal Daddy in heaven.

It was almost three o'clock in the morning when Michael prayed to receive Christ into his heart. He offered me some tea and I counseled him regarding what he needed to tell ZeZe the next day. I told him to explain what the Lord had done for him tonight and tell her that he would not convert to Islam as planned. I told him that he needed to tell her to read the gospels for herself and learn about Jesus. I encouraged him to stay faithful to the Lord so that perhaps ZeZe would also come to know Him and receive Him as her Savior.

As I left his house we hugged each other again. I asked him to bring ZeZe to my church because I wanted her to meet the women there who were Muslim by birth and had received Christ. I assured him that they had a great testimony and that meeting them and hearing their stories would touch her heart. Some of the women in particular had been very strict, fanatical-type, Muslims and they had dramatic testimonies.

He agreed to ask her to come to church with him. I gave him the address and left his home rejoicing. I was so happy that God saw fit to use me to bring Michael the good news of the gospel and that he was indeed ready to receive his Savior. I thanked the Lord with all of my heart for saving him and I prayed for ZeZe to come also to know the Lord. I was looking forward to seeing what would transpire in ZeZe's life after this.

It was surprising to see Michael and ZeZe attending my church the following Sunday. I rejoiced to see both of them and I introduced them to my friends. I made sure that ZeZe met one of the faithful Muslim ladies who had converted to Christianity. I left her with this lady and I took Michael aside. I asked him how he convinced ZeZe to come to church. He said that the next day, after he had accepted Christ, he told her everything that had happened to him. He explained to her that he could not renounce Christ in order to marry her. He shared with her my story about how I was born Muslim and had come to know Christ as my Savior. ZeZe was so skeptical that she wanted to come to the church to see the Muslim converts herself.

Later that day we met again and I asked ZeZe how she liked the church. She said she was very happy and at the same time was amazed that she was seeing and talking with Muslims who had converted to Christianity.

ZeZe started meeting regularly with one of the Muslim convert women. After a few weeks she accepted Christ and was baptized at our church. Praise the Lord who is faithful to His word! As we are told in the Scriptures, **"If we endure, we shall also reign with Him. If we deny Him, He also will deny us. If we are faithless, He remains faithful; He cannot deny Himself"** (2 Timothy 2:12-13). Later, Michael and ZeZe left Egypt and married in a foreign country.

## A VISIT FROM THE SECRET POLICE

Before Michael and ZeZe left Egypt, Michael and I would often attend church together. He always accompanied me whenever I was asked to speak in churches and we became very close friends. One day, after one of the church meetings, Michael and I took a taxi to go home. As was our usual practice, we would sit together in the back seat of the taxi and discuss the sermon. We would speak loud enough for the driver and other passengers to hear our conversation. This was our way of witnessing as we traveled to our destinations.

Michael and I lived fairly close to each other and on this particular taxi ride he was dropped off first. After he got out of the taxi I gave the taxi driver a tract and shared a little more with him about Jesus. While I was speaking with him, I somehow felt that I should not reveal my address. So I had him drop me off a couple of blocks away from my house, and when he was out of sight I walked the rest of the way home.

A few days later, I received a notice in the mail from the secret police asking me to come to their office. When I arrived, I met with an officer who asked me some questions about my family and my background. He asked me why I had converted, so I told him. He also wanted to know which church I attended and had been baptized in.

When he learned about my family and their status in the government, he allowed me to go home with no further questioning. Before I left his office I asked him how he obtained my name and address, but he would not tell me.

Later that day, I met with Michael who told me that the secret police had called him and questioned him about me. They wanted to know how we met and what kind of a relationship we had. Michael was afraid and he told them everything. He also gave them my address.

Michael expressed sorrow for having revealed so much to the police. He asked me to forgive him. I encouraged him by telling him that my life was in God's hands and not in the hands of any human being.

Later, I realized that the taxi driver was the one who had called the secret police. Since he did not know my address he gave them Michael's. I believe Satan was very angry about the salvation of Michael and ZeZe, and this was his way of trying to stop me from witnessing. But I was not intimidated. This was my first encounter with the secret police before my imprisonment.

Both Michael and ZeZe continued to grow in their faith. After their departure from Egypt, they married and had several children. God has blessed their lives and they are both being used by the Lord in their adopted country.

*"The name of the LORD is a strong tower; the righteous run to it and are safe."*

*Proverbs 18:10*

# 5

# Mysterious Disappearances

I remember December 19, 1981 very clearly. The events of this day would make a great impact on my life. I was in a taxi traveling to the center of Cairo. I was carrying some tracts called "The most shocking accident in the world." The tracts explained how the true believers in Christ will suddenly disappear in what appears like a mysterious accident. Millions of believers in Christ will be snatched from the earth. Christ will take them to protect them from a terrible judgment that will effect the whole world. I handed each of the passengers in the taxi a tract. Everyone started reading the tract and began to ask me about it. I shared with them about Jesus from both the Qur'an and the Bible. I told them that Jesus (Issa, the son of Mary) is the Mighty God who came to die for our sins and guarantee a place for us in heaven. I told them that Jesus will come again to take (rapture) all those who receive Him as Savior to live with Him forever. This will happen in the twinkle of an eye as the Scripture says, **"Behold, I tell you a mystery: We shall not all sleep, but we shall**

all be changed- in a moment, in the twinkling of an eye, at the last trumpet. For the trumpet will sound and the dead will be raised incorruptible, and we shall be changed" (1 Corinthians 15:51-52).

After answering many questions, the passengers were dropped off at their destination and I was left alone with the driver. The driver asked me, "Why are you talking to us about Jesus? We are Muslims and we don't change our religion. Did you ever meet any Muslim who changed his religion to become a Christian?"

"Yes, I know many Muslims who have become Christians."

He smiled and challenged me by saying, "If you show me one Muslim who became a Christian, I will convert and go to church with you."

I replied, "I am. I was a Muslim and now I am a Christian."

He did not believe me and said, "You are only saying this to try to convert me, you must be joking."

Immediately I remembered the Scripture where King Festus in the Bible said to Paul, **"You are beside yourself! Much learning is driving you mad!"** (Acts 26:24).

I showed the taxi driver my Egyptian ID which stated my full name as "Mohammed Kamel" and my religion as "Muslim." He was shocked when he saw this. I asked him if he would come to the church meeting as he had agreed. He replied, "Of course." He took down the name and address of the meeting place and said he would be there for the evening service. I left his car rejoicing.

We would gather regularly for the mid-week evening service in the neighborhood of Doqy's. This was the address that I had given to the taxi driver and I hoped to see him later that evening.

Instead of coming to the meeting he went to the headquarters of Mr. Nabaou Ishmael, the Minister of Internal Security. He told Mr. Ishmael that he learned of a group that "threatened to turn Egypt upside down" by trying to convert Muslims to Christianity. Based on this information, Mr. Ishmael contacted the Egyptian Secret Service and I was arrested immediately.

*"So they departed from the presence of the council, rejoicing that they were counted worthy to suffer shame for His name."*

*Acts 5:41*

# 6

# The Egyptian Secret Service Chief

It was close to ten o'clock when Mr. Alaa finally finished questioning me. He pushed a buzzer, summoning a guard. When the guard came to take me out, I paused and reminded Mr. Alaa, "You promised to keep me for a half hour and then let me go." It was now over two hours later, and I was still being detained.

He responded by saying, "I do not have permission to release you, only the Minister of Internal Security, Mr. Nabaou Ishmael, has that authority. I am sending you to Mr. Nabael Eita, the High Chief of the Egyptian Secret Service for further questioning."

Upon hearing this, I asked him, "May I call my family, they will be concerned about me."

"Give me their phone number and I will notify them," he said.

On the way to the detaining room the guard asked me, "What did you do?"

I told him, "I was a Muslim who became a Christian."

"Son, why did you do that?" the guard replied. "You are still in your youth. You have cut your life short. Don't you know that everyone who comes to this place never comes out?"

The guard took me to an underground room, called the hagz, which is a detention cell. The concrete cell was dark and damp. There was a wooden bench about twenty inches deep mounted on the wall. Nothing else was in the room. It was the month of December and it was very cold. My teeth were chattering when the guard locked the heavy door behind me. I shivered for some time before I knocked on the door to ask if I could have a blanket but the guard refused my request. I spent the first night without a cover. I didn't know then, but in the very near future I would spend many nights this way.

My first night I began praying and worshipping the Lord. I gave thanks to the Lord for allowing me to participate in suffering for the sake of His Name. As I was worshipping, I felt the power of the Holy Spirit come upon me and I was filled with great joy. I was honored that God considered me worthy of proclaiming Him before those in authority in a Muslim country. I felt the Holy Spirit encouraging me and strengthening me with power to overcome the extremity of my surroundings. I was able to fall into a deep sleep until I heard my cell door unlock the next morning.

I thought that the guard had come to release me, but instead, he had orders. "You are going to meet with Mr. Nabael Eita, the Egyptian Secret Service High Chief." We walked until we arrived at his office. As the guard opened the door I saw a middle aged man standing behind a desk, dressed in a suit. He was not very tall but he had an intimidating presence about him. Mr. Eita motioned for me to take the seat in front of his desk. The guard saluted him then left the room.

Mr. Eita introduced himself to me as the director of the Egyptian Secret Service. Then he asked me, "Why have you changed your religion?" I shared with him what I had shared with Mr. Alaa the day before. Before I could say much he began to violently pound his desk. The room seemed to shake each time his fist met his desk. "You are an infidel! The punishment for an infidel is death!"

Each time his fist hit the desk, he yelled, "I will kill you! I will kill you! You will be branded, and I will stick a hose in you in places that they don't belong!" he threatened. "You are crazy! I have never before heard of a Muslim becoming a Christian!"

"Don't you know that in an Islamic country Sharia law commands you to be put to death!" he said. "Do you know that I have the power and authority to torture you until you forget your name? Do you reject our prophet?" he continued.

The Egyptian Secret Service chief began lecturing me about Islam and how the prophet Muhammad was the last prophet that came from God. He told me that whoever doesn't believe in Islam will go to hell and have eternal punishment.

I responded by asking him, "Have you ever read the Bible?"

He shouted at me when I said this and started to make fun of the Bible. He said emphatically, "We are born as Muslims, we will live as Muslims, and we will die as Muslims. I know many Christians that have converted to Islam, but never have I ever heard or even seen any Muslim convert to Christianity!"

Mr. Eita changed the subject. He began asking me about other Muslims who had converted to Christianity. I could see that he was trying to get information from me and I did not want to bring harm to my brothers and sisters in Christ, so I chose to remain silent. When he saw that he could not get any information, he began verbally abusing me again, calling me a crazy man and an infidel for following Christ.

I knew then that I was not going to be released so I asked him, "Can someone notify my family of where I am?"

"Only under one condition," he said. "You must renounce your faith in Christ and return to Islam. Then we will release you as a free man. Until then, you are "Kafir" (an infidel), under the penalty of Sharia law, and your blood is without price."

But I was not afraid. I felt the Lord standing next to me, **"But the Lord stood with me and strengthened me, so that the message might be preached fully through me…"** (2 Timothy 4:17).

*"Nor is there salvation in any other, for there is no other name under heaven given among men by which we must be saved."*

*Acts 4:12*

# 7

# Why I left Islam

When Mr. Eita calmed down I started to share with him the mystery of Jesus that has been hidden from Muslims for ages. I explained how this mystery has the power to change lives. I told him that I was born into a Muslim family. We were dutiful Muslims. I described the commitment my family had to Islam.

"I earnestly desired to please Allah. I was seeking purity and cleansing from my sins. I read the Qur'an everyday. I woke up early to wash (wudu) and perform the morning prayers. At four o'clock in the morning, I would splash cold water on my face, hands and feet to prepare myself. Sometimes I would pray even more than five times a day, trying to get closer to Allah. I would cry out to Allah to forgive me of my sins and change me into a clean person. I wanted to be pure from sin. I wanted to please Allah."

Mr. Eita listened intently to what I was saying.

I continued, "I hated my sins and I would continually confess my sins to Allah. As I prayed I would promise not to sin again, and for a few days I would be good, but not for long. This happened many times, over and over. I pleaded with Allah to make me pure and give me the strength to be good. From the outside, it might have appeared that I was a righteous person, but on the inside I was not. My thoughts were sinful and when no one was watching I would commit the sins that I detested. I would cry desperately to Allah to help me conquer my sins, but nothing changed. I was like a man beating the air."

"All my prayers and acts of devotion to Allah were in vain. After a few years I gave up trying to be a good Muslim and simply went through the motions. I continued the ritual prayers and other obligations of Islam, but I had lost all hope that Allah could change me."

I grew more and more confident in how I spoke with Mr. Eita. I did not care that he could hurt me. I could not stay silent in my love for the Lord. I told him, "When I discovered that God loved me and sent Jesus to pay for my sin with His life and death, God began to work in my heart. He began to change me from the inside. It was so refreshing and different from anything I had ever experienced. I had never known anything so beautiful. I never could have imagined relating to God in this way. I never could have dreamt that God would want to relate to me. Instead of feeling guilty and trapped, I was forgiven and free. I had new life and new hope."

## Difference Between Islam and Christianity

Mr. Eita sat in shock. I suspected that there were not many men who had challenged him in such a way. I could tell from his increasing anger that he didn't know how to handle such disregard for his authority. I explained to Mr. Eita, "The essential difference between Christianity and Islam is how we go about obtaining favor with God. In Islam the focus is on our trying to change ourselves by performing certain ritual acts. We pray five times and day, we perform ritual bathing, we wear certain clothes and abstain from certain foods. We do all this in the hope that we will please Allah and become good. In Christianity our focus is on allowing God to change us from within so that we will be set free from our desire to sin."

"Only God has the power to change us and free us from the power of sin. Only He has the power to make our hearts clean. We cannot accomplish this in our own strength no matter how hard we try. In Christianity, Jesus promises to change us as we put our trust in Him. The Bible says, "**I give you a new heart, and put a new spirit within you; and I will take the heart of stone out of your flesh and I give you a heart of flesh. I will put My Spirit within you and cause you to walk in My statutes, and you will keep My judgments and do them**" (Ezekiel 36:26-27).

I urged Mr. Eita to pay attention to the words: "**give, put, take** and **cause**. These are action words. And it is God who is doing the acting, not man! God knows we are powerless to change ourselves so He says He will do it! He will save us, He will change us and He will cause us to walk in His ways. He is the One who will act on our behalf to **take** away our stony hearts and **put** a new spirit within us. From the start to the finish, God is the one who is saving and purifying us."

I told him, "I know many Muslims, scholars and friends who think and believe that with good tradition and moral guidance, we can change ourselves. They are mistakenly optimistic because they are ignorant of our human nature. The reality is that we need a radical solution which will transform our nature. Our efforts or works cannot save us from the bondage of sin or the power of Satan. We need a Savior!"

Mr. Eita listened quietly with a scowl on his face. I was expecting him to interrupt me with an angry outburst at any moment. I decided to share a very powerful and important experience from the beginning of my Christian life.

In August, 1979, two months after accepting Christ as my Savior, I went to a Christian conference at King Mariout Camp in Alexandria. I remember a pastor sharing about the power Jesus had to change the human heart. He kept repeating the words of the apostle Paul, "**...Christ Jesus came into the world to save sinners, of whom I am chief**" (1 Timothy 1:15). The preacher stressed that we are all spiritually sick and slaves to sin's control over us. Even the great apostle Paul tells us that he was a terrible sinner until he experienced Christ's changing power. The Scriptures also states, **"They have all turned aside, they have together become corrupt; there is none that does good, no, not one"** (Psalms 14:3). All people are infected by sin. No human being is exempt from its power.

The pastor shared a story from the Gospel of Mark (See Mark 5:1-15) about a man who lived among the tombs. He was tormented by a host of evil spirits living inside of him.

The demons (evil spirits) were shaking with fear when they saw Jesus. The demons bowed down to Jesus when they saw Him coming. They begged Him not to torment them. They knew exactly who Jesus was, the Son of the Most High God. There were two thousand demons in this man and they quaked in His presence. The demons knew that Jesus had authority to do with them as He pleased.

When Jesus commanded the evil spirits to come out of the man they went into the pigs that were feeding nearby. The evil spirits had no choice but to obey Him. They entered the swine and as the swine fled down a steep slope, they drowned in the sea.

This is a graphic picture of what happened to mankind after the fall in the Garden of Eden. All of us have become slaves to Satan. We are all slaves to darkness, cutting ourselves day and night, as it were, with sinful acts. We see in the story how no one could control this man, not even with chains. The same is true regarding our sins. Even the strongest chains cannot tame our sinful nature.

The good news is that there is One who does have the power to break the control of sin over us. It is Jesus Christ, the Son of the Most High God! His radical power can break the stronghold of sin. Jesus has authority over Satan to release us from sin's grip.

At the end of this story, we see that Jesus delivers the demon possessed man. The man is no longer a slave to the demons inside of him. We see the Scriptures tell us that he was, "…**in his right mind.**" In the book of Acts we read, "…**God anointed Jesus of Nazareth with the Holy Spirit and with power, who went about doing good and healing all who were**

**oppressed by the devil…"** (Acts 10:38).

## SET FREE

As this speaker continued to preach, I was touched by the Holy Spirit. My heart burned within me while he spoke. I began to realize that there was great hope for me and my struggles with sin. I knelt down by the sofa where I was sitting and I started to pray a simple prayer. I said, "Lord, if this preacher is telling the truth about Jesus, please change me." I kept repeating this many times. "Please God, if you are Jesus, change me, change me, change me." Suddenly it seemed like there was a heavenly shower that poured over me. A flood of the Holy Spirit filled me from the inside out.

There were two people sitting on the sofa with me, one on either side. We felt the sofa shake and I began speaking in a strange language. I knew it was not Arabic. It seemed to be a heavenly language. I was praising God in the spirit with great joy. I continued praising God with all my heart and soul. I never experienced this before in my life. At this very moment I felt a great freedom in my spirit. I felt the chains of darkness fall off. I gave thanks to God for delivering me from Satan's bondage. The light of Christ filled my heart. I saw anew how much God loves me. I felt that I was very precious in His sight.

That day, I knew that I had become a new creature in Christ. I felt the fire of the Holy Spirit purifying me and filling me with the ability to live according to the righteous statutes of God. I found in myself the power to reject the sins that had so easily entangled me. I stopped smoking cigarettes. I stopped cussing and chasing after girls. I started to feel like a new man was living in me, that the old one was gone. My life became calm and I was filled with peace, joy and love, even for my enemies. My heart became bold and courageous even in difficult situations. The apostle Paul describes it like this, **"Therefore, if anyone is in Christ, he is a new creation; old things have passed away; behold, all things have become new"** (2 Corinthians 5:17). From that day on, Jesus put a new song in my mouth. He put my feet on the Solid Rock. He set my spirit free from evil longings and Satan's grip.

I told Mr. Eita, "This is why I became a follower of Jesus (Issa). This is why I am standing before you, testifying of the things that Jesus has done for me and will do for anyone who calls on His name!"

After I finished telling this story to Mr. Eita, I asked him, "Do you have a copy of the Bible?" He opened his desk and pulled out a Bible. I took it from his hand and opened to the book of Acts. I read to him the words of the apostle Peter when he spoke of Jesus saying, **"Nor is there salvation in any other, for there is no other name under heaven given among men by which we must be saved"** (Acts 4:12).

I pointed him to the words on the page where it says, **"No other name under heaven given among men by which we must be saved."** I told him, "It is only through the name of Jesus Christ that any man or woman can be saved and released from the curse of sin, inherited from his ancestors, Adam and Eve."

Mr. Eita seemed disturbed that there was nothing he could do to deter me from my love for Jesus. I knew that no matter how angry he became that I would not stop. God revealed the truth to me and there was no turning back.

*"But God demonstrates His own love toward us,
in that while we were still sinners, Christ died for us."*

*Romans 5:8*

# 8

# The Crucifixion: Fact or Fiction

I prayed that God would open a door to give me an opportunity to witness to Mr. Eita. While sharing with Mr. Eita about the changing power of Christ, I began to explain to him the necessity of Christ's death and resurrection. I quoted the Scriptures where the apostle Paul tells us, **"But God demonstrates His love toward us, in that while we were still sinners, Christ died for us"** (Romans 5:8). God's love demands that Jesus must die in our place because we are all infected with sin. The Scriptures declare, **"For the wages of sin is death, but the gift of God is eternal life through Christ Jesus our Lord"** (Romans 6:23).

I explained to him that God deeply loves us and does not want us to perish. The Scriptures tell us, **"The Lord...is not willing that any should perish but that all should come to repentance"** (2 Peter 3:9). We are also told that God takes no pleasure in the wicked being condemned to hell, for He says, **"...I have no pleasure in the death of the wicked, but that the wicked turn from his way and live..."** (Ezekiel 33:11).

I could tell Mr. Eita was curious about what I was saying. He could not mask that through his anger and threats. So I explained about the principle of God's holiness. "God is completely holy. There is no sin or imperfections in God, and because of this, no sin, imperfections or uncleanness can enter His presence. We are without hope unless God provides a way for us to become clean before Him. God's judgment requires that we spend eternity in hell as the penalty for our sins. If God let us into His heaven in our sinful condition, then God would be associating Himself with evil. While God is completely righteous and just, He is also completely loving and merciful. He longs to have a relationship with those He has created. Sin must be dealt with in order for God and man to have a relationship."

"Mr. Eita," I asked, "What would happen in a criminal jail if the jailer, because he had a sensitive heart and felt sorry for the prisoners, decided to let all the prisoners out of the jail? Would this be a good thing?"

"Certainly not!" he declared.

"So how can we expect God to do that with sinners who have broken His holy laws? If God did not demand payment for our sins this would nullify God's righteousness. God does not act like a human being. He is the Great Judge and His holiness will judge all sinners, including you and me."

I asked Mr. Eita, "How is it possible that God can be a God of justice and mercy at the same time? How could a God of justice erase my debt, so I would not have to pay for my sins in the eternity of hell, and still be a just God?

There was silence for a few seconds and then he asked me, "How?"

"It is only by the cross of Christ. God sent Jesus Christ, who is called the 'Word' in the Qur'an (Q 4:171), to be the redeemer of mankind. God sent Jesus in the flesh to live a sinless, perfect life and then die on the cross in our place. I quoted what Paul said in Ephesians, **'(We) were by nature children of wrath, just as the others. But God, who is rich in mercy, because of His great love with which He loved us, even when** we were dead in trespasses, made us alive together with Christ…and raised us up together, and made us sit together in heavenly places in Christ Jesus' (Ephesians 2:3-6)."

I knew he was listening, so I continued, "Jesus took the punishment for us by His death on the cross and this satisfied God's justice bringing reconciliation. The Bible calls this, 'The gift of God' (Ephesians 2:8). And what a great gift this is! Only God's Son was able to satisfy God's demands for justice. When Jesus died on the cross, the Bible tells us that He took upon Himself the sins of all mankind. This means that every single sin that has ever been committed past, present and future by every human being who has ever lived or is yet to be born, was poured into the body of Jesus as He hung on the cross. Jesus, who lived a perfectly sinless life, took upon Himself the anguish of the sins of the world in order to satisfy God's righteous demands. He descended into the grave and then He rose from the dead on the third day, sealing salvation for all who believe. It is recorded, '…Christ died for our sins according to the Scriptures…He was buried, and that He rose again the third day…' (1 Corinthians 15:3-4). This is how God satisfied His demand for justice while at the same time proving and confirming His great love for us. Again, we are told, 'For He (God) made Him (Jesus) who knew no sin to be sin for us, that we might become the righteousness of God in Him' (2 Corinthians 5:21)."

"Praise be to God, Mr. Eita!"

## THE QUR'AN AND THE MOMENTOUS SACRIFICE

In the Bible, Christ's death on the cross for our sins is called the principle of redemption. To explain this to Mr. Eita, I referred to the story of Abraham from the Qur'an. In the Qur'an, Abraham is said to have had a dream where God told him to offer his son as a sacrifice. Just as Abraham lifted his hand to do this, God called out to him. The Qur'an says, "We call out to him: 'O Abraham! Thou hast already fulfilled the vision'…then We (Allah) ransomed him (Abraham's son) with a **momentous sacrifice**" (Q37:104-107).

In the Bible this is real story and not a dream. Just as

Abraham was about to slay his son, God stopped him saying, **"Do not lay your hand on the lad, or do anything to him...Abraham lifted his eyes, and looked, and there behind him was a ram caught in a thicket by its horns. So Abraham went and took the ram, and offered it up for a burnt offering instead of his son"** (Genesis 22:12-13). It is clear that God saved Abraham's son by providing another sacrifice (the ram). The story of Abraham and his son is a precursor to what God did for us through Christ on a grand scale. Instead of God punishing us, He had His own Son pay the price.

Dear reader, please pay attention to these four words: **momentous, sacrifice, ransomed** and **instead**. These words explain what Jesus did for us through His crucifixion. He was our ransom. He was our sacrifice. He took the place of our deserved punishment instead of us even though He was completely innocent. Jesus died as our substitute (ransom) the same way the ram was a substitute for Abraham's son.

I asked Mr. Eita, "Can you tell me what the Qur'an means by the words, 'momentous sacrifice?'" Seeing that he was having a difficult time trying to answer me I answered the question for him. I said, "'momentous' means 'universal, mighty, or beyond estimation.' It is obvious that the ram could not be a momentous or a universal sacrifice. The Qur'an was referring to a mighty universal unlimited sacrifice which would be sufficient in quality to redeem all of mankind."

"Mr. Eita, where can we find such a 'momentous sacrifice?'"

"I don't know," he responded quietly.

I told him, "The momentous sacrifice was referring to Jesus' death on the cross. John the Baptist (YahYah), declared, **'Behold! The Lamb (ram) of God who takes away the sin of the world!'** (John 1:29). The apostle Peter says it this way, **'...You were not redeemed with corruptible things, like silver or gold, from your aimless conduct received by tradition from your fathers, but with the precious blood of Christ, as of a lamb without blemish and without spot'** (1 Peter 1:18-19)."

I continued by saying, "Because God loves us, He sent the

Messiah (Al-Masih) who is Jesus (Issa) as an unlimited sacrifice. God sent Jesus to die on our behalf; on my behalf and on yours, Mr. Eita. This was the price for our ransom. Now, because of this ransom the Bible tells us, 'Whoever believes in Him (Jesus) should not perish, but have everlasting life' (John 3:16)."

## SUBSTITUTION THEORY

After hearing my words, Mr. Eita abruptly interrupted me and said, "Why do you say that Jesus died when the Qur'an says that he did not die?" He quoted, "That they said (in boast), 'We killed Christ Jesus, the son of Mary, the Messenger of Allah', but **they killed him not, nor crucified him**. Only a **likeness** of that was shown to them" (Q 4:157).

Mr. Eita said to me, "We Muslims know that Issa (Jesus) never died. God honored him so much that he lifted Issa to heaven while he was still alive. As Issa was lifted to heaven, Allah tricked the Romans by causing Judah (Judas Iscariot) to look like Issa. The Romans, believing that Judah was Issa, took Judah to the cross and had him crucified instead. It was not Issa they put on the cross. Issa never died."

I replied, "I am familiar with this teaching of Islam, called the **Substitution Theory,** because this is what Muslims are taught regarding the crucifixion. But I have a hard time believing this theory for several reasons."

"First of all, Mr. Eita, there are verses in the Qur'an that state just the opposite." I quoted for him the verse which states, **_"Peace is on me (Issa) the day I was born, and the day I die, and the day I shall be raised to life (again)!"_** (Q 19:33). Then I quoted another verse where Allah states, **"Behold! 'O Jesus! I will take thee and raise thee to Myself...'"** (Q 3:55, 5:117). The English words, _I will take thee_, are translated from the Arabic words, _Inni mutawafika_. In Arabic, this phrase means **_I will cause you to die._** The Qur'an teaches of Issa's death as well as his resurrection. So I asked Mr. Eita, "Why does the Qur'an contradict itself? Can a book that contradicts itself really be the words of God?"

"Secondly, lying and deception are contrary to the character of God. God does not lie and He does not deceive. The Bible tells us, **'God is not a man that He should lie…"** (Numbers 23: 19). In fact we are told that God *cannot* lie (Titus 1:2). The Substitution Theory contradicts the very essence and nature of God."

"Thirdly, even if it was true that God wanted Issa to escape death, wouldn't it have made more sense for Him to have 'lifted' Jesus in the presence of witnesses? This would have brought more honor to Issa than doing it secretly." I reminded Mr. Eita, "God saved the Jews from the Egyptian Pharaohs by doing many miracles and by opening up the Red Sea for them. These acts weren't done in secret, but for all to see, and the whole world learned of these miracles."

"I also suggest, Mr. Eita, that it makes no sense for God to trick the Romans. God is a loving God, so why would He hurt Jesus' devoted disciples (al-hawariyun) and relatives by causing them to witness a terrible crucifixion that had no purpose? And what about the multitudes of people throughout history that believe that Jesus was crucified for their sins? Do you think a just and honorable God would allow this without it being true? Do you think that God delights in seeing millions of people deceived?"

"Fourthly," I asked Mr. Eita, "How is it that 575 years after Christ, Muhammad could say that our Lord Jesus Christ was not crucified? The birth and crucifixion of Christ were well-documented long before Muhammad was born. We all know that the Roman Empire was ruling the entire world when Jesus was on the earth and that crucifixion was used for capital offenses. There is an abundance of evidence that the crucifixion of Jesus did, in fact, take place. We know from the documents of the esteemed Jewish historian Flavius Josephus (AD 37-100) that Pilate, the Roman governor, ordered Jesus' crucifixion, and that was carried out in the presence of many eye witnesses."[1]

"In addition to all this," I explained, "There are many hundreds of prophecies in the Old Testament Scriptures that predicted that the Messiah would die. These Old Testament prophecies were written hundreds of years before Jesus was born. These prophecies are accurate even to the smallest detail which the New Testament writers and ancient historians confirm for us."

I shared with Mr. Eita the following examples. The Old Testament book of Isaiah, written 500 years before the birth of Jesus, says, **"Surely He has borne our grief and carried our sorrows; yet we esteemed Him stricken, smitten by God, and afflicted. But He was wounded for our transgressions, He was bruised for our iniquities; the chastisement for our peace was upon Him, and by His stripes we are healed"** (Isaiah 53:4-5). In the New Testament, the apostle Peter, who was an eye witness to the crucifixion, confirms the fulfillment of Isaiah's prophecy. He states, **"Who Himself (Jesus) bore our sins in His own body on the tree (cross), that we, having died to sins, might live for righteousness - by his stripes you were healed"** (1 Peter 2:24).

I spoke of another Old Testament prophet, Zechariah, who gave a prophecy regarding the price that would be given to Jesus' betrayer. He writes, **"Then I (the betrayer) said to them, 'If it is agreeable to you, give me my wages;'...So they weighed out for my wages thirty pieces of silver. And the LORD said to me, 'Throw it to the potter' — the princely price they set on me! So I took the thirty pieces of silver and threw them into the house of the LORD for the potter"** (Zechariah 11:12-13). In the New Testament we see that this was fulfilled. The Gospel of Matthew records, **"Then one of the twelve, called Judas Iscariot, went to the chief priests and asked, 'What are you willing to give me if I deliver Him to you?' And they counted out for him thirty pieces of silver. So from that time he sought opportunity to betray Him"** (Matthew 26:14-16). **"When morning came, all the chief priests and elders of the people plotted against Jesus to put Him to death. And when they had bound Him, they led Him away and delivered Him to Pontius Pilate the governor. Then Judas, His betrayer, seeing that He had been condemned, was remorseful and brought back the thirty pieces of silver to the chief priests and elders, saying, 'I have sinned by betraying innocent blood.' And they said, 'What is that to us? You see to it!' Then he threw down the pieces of silver in the temple and departed, and went and hanged himself. But the chief priests took the silver pieces and said, 'It is not lawful to put them into the treasury, because they are the price of blood.' And they consulted together and bought with them the potter's field, to bury strangers in"** (Matthew 27:1-7).

"Mr. Eita, the prophets Isaiah and Zechariah gave these prophecies 500 years before the Messiah was born, and they came to pass exactly as God had declared they would. Why would God bother giving these prophecies regarding the Messiah's impending death if they weren't significant or if He didn't intend to fulfill them?"

At this, Mr. Eita was outraged. He began to curse me and threaten to beat me as he was pounding the desk before him. "May Allah curse you for such betrayal!"

*"And I heard a loud voice from heaven saying, 'The tabernacle of God is with men, and He will dwell with them, and they shall be His people. God Himself will be with them and be their God.'"*

*Revelation 21:3*

# 9

# The Undercover Agent

Mr. Eita called one of his secret agents to come in. "Take him back to the hagz!" he yelled. I spent the next three nights in a small, dark, underground room.

On the fourth day in the hagz, at about eleven o'clock at night, I heard the door open. A man dressed in the clothing of an Imam was brought to my cell by a guard. He had been arrested and placed under surveillance. He asked me about my family and also about my name.

He complemented me on my name saying, "What a great privilege to be born on the same day as the prophet and also named after him." He sat next to me on the bench and started asking me questions, "Why have you been detained?"

I told him how I met Christ and became a new person. After listening, he responded, "All Christians are infidels! Their book is unclean. Islam is the only true religion."

When I sensed that he was not sent to my cell as a prisoner, but rather to spy on me and convert me back to Islam, I decided to change the direction of the conversation. I began asking him pointed questions about some of Muhammad's practices.

"Why did Muhammad, at the age of fifty-four, take Aisha, a seven year old child to be his wife?" We were both familiar with the account of Aisha's betrothal.

He responded by saying, "Aisha was actually much older in age, she was not as young as you think, Muhammed would never desire a child."

I quickly reminded the Imam, "The Hadith clearly states that Aisha was nine years old when Muhammed finally married her." Aisha recounts the story in the Hadith. "My mother came to me while I was playing in the swing…She took me down, then she combed my hair and washed my face with some water, then she took me inside to the prophet of Allah and he was sitting on the bed in our home. Then she set me in his lap…then the people and the women left the room…the prophet of Allah slept with me in my home and I was a nine year old girl."[2]

"Muhammad agreed to marry Aisha to please Abu Bakr, who was to be the first successor to Islam."

I exclaimed, "Do you think it is natural for a fifty-four year old man to have relations with a nine year old?"

The Imam quickly jumped to Muhammad's defense again claiming, "She was given as a gift from her father, who was a close friend of Muhammad's. He merely accepted her so as not to offend his friend."

The Imam only became angry with me as I discredited everything he was claiming. I continued my questioning asking, "Why did the prophet Muhammed coerce his adopted son Zaid Bin Haritha to divorce his young wife Zaynab Bint Jahsh so that he could have her? Why weren't the many wives he already had enough to satisfy him?"

The Imam argued, "Muhammad married many widows as a charity since they had no one to care for them. The prophet made marriages to form alliances with different tribes. This was a great service to the cause and spread of Islam."

"She was not a widow and he didn't need her to form an alliance. Why did none of the other prophets, such as Moses or Jesus, use the practice of polygamy to spread religion?"

The Imam had no response.

I steered the conversation to the concept of heaven in Islam. "I cannot trust a prophet that attracts his followers through the lure of fleshly desires. Tell me, how many women is it that Allah will offer to the faithful Muslim men in heaven?"

"Seventy-two women," he replied.

"And what kind of women are they?" I asked.

"Houris," he replied, which in Arabic means, beautiful virgins. "The houris are so magnificent that you can see their shining bodies through seven layers of clothing. Even after they have intercourse they return to being virgins again and again so they never spoil."

"The heaven of Islam seems more to me like a brothel than a holy place" I commented.

I knew from my studies that the heaven of Islam offered the men of Arabia everything they could not have in life. The heaven of Islam is described as being a garden filled with lush dates, pomegranates and other fruits. It is pictured as being flooded with rivers of fresh water, **honey, milk, liquor, and beautiful women**. These are all the things that life could not produce for these desert dwellers. The following verses are some of the descriptions made in the Qur'an,

"(Here is) a Parable of the Garden which the righteous are promised: in it are rivers of water incorruptible; rivers of milk of which the taste never changes; rivers of wine, a joy to those who drink; and rivers of honey pure and clear. In it there are for them all kinds of fruits; and Grace from their Lord. (Can those in such Bliss) be compared to such as shall dwell forever in the Fire, and be given, to drink, boiling water, so that it cuts up their bowels (to pieces)?" (Q 47:15).

"There will be two Gardens- Containing all kinds (of trees and delights)...In them (each) will be two Springs flowing (free)... In them will be Fruits of every kind, two and two... They (righteous Muslims) will recline on Carpets, whose inner linings will be of rich brocade... the Fruit of the Gardens will be near (and easy of reach)... In them will be (Maidens), chaste, restraining their glances, whom no man or Jinn before them has touched... Like unto Rubies and coral. Reclining on green Cushions and rich Carpets of beauty" (Q 55:46-76).

Muhammad used these attractions to entice many followers because they were ignorant of the fact that these same pleasures were found naturally in other parts of the world. His followers were even ready to die for the pleasures of Islam's heaven as some still are today. Other verses in the Qur'an even offer *children* to the Muslim faithful to be used for sexual pleasure. The Qur'an states, "(They will be) on Thrones encrusted (with gold and precious stones), Reclining on them, facing each other. Round about them will (serve) **youths** of perpetual (freshness), with goblets, (shining) beakers, and cups (filled) out of clear-flowing fountains: No after-ache will they receive there from, nor will they suffer intoxication: And the flesh of fowls, any that they may desire. And (there will be) **Companions** with beautiful, big, and lustrous eyes, Like unto Pearls well-guarded. A reward for the deeds of their past (life)" (Q 56:15-24).

According to Muhammad, Muslim men will be surrounded with every earthly pleasure imaginable. They will be satisfying themselves on chaste women, on sumptuous foods and delicacies, and drinking the finest liquor. They will be indulging their fleshly appetites forever and they will be doing this, according to Muhammad, all in the presence of God. Can this be so? Is God's heaven a night club? Certainly not! For God is holy and nothing unholy can ever enter God's presence! The Bible tells us, **"(God dwells) in unapproachable light"** (1 Timothy 6:16). It also tells us, **"If any one defiles the temple of God, God will destroy him. For the temple of God is holy..."** (1 Corinthians 3:17).

I explained to the Imam, "Jesus describes heaven very differently from the heaven Muhammad describes." I referenced the following verses:

**"There shall by no means enter it anything that defiles, or causes an abomination or a lie, but only those who are written in the Lamb's Book of Life"** (Revelation 21:27).

**"Behold, the tabernacle of God is with men, and He will dwell with them, and they shall be His people"** (Revelation 21:3).

**"…There shall be no more death, nor sorrow, nor crying. There shall be no more pain, for the former things have passed away"** (Revelation 21:4-5).

I told him, "The real heaven is the place where God dwells with redeemed mankind. There will be no more death, marriage or sex. God's throne is a holy place where sin does not enter. It is not a place for sleeping with women and drinking liquor."

He told me, **"You are an infidel!** Allah, please forgive me for listening to these words!" Then he knocked on the door for the guard to let him out of my cell. The guard quickly came to unlock the door for him. I knew then that my suspicions about him had been correct. He was not a prisoner, but was sent as an informant. But praise the Lord, the One living in me is greater than the one that is against me. **"…He who is in you is greater than he who is in the world"** (1 John 4:4).

*"If you are reproached for the name of Christ, blessed are you, for the Spirit of glory and of God rests upon you. On their part He is blasphemed, but on your part He is glorified."*

*1 Peter 4:14*

# 10

# Transfer to the Deputy Attorney General

The morning of my fourth day in the hagz, I woke up to the sound of footsteps approaching my cell. Suddenly the door opened and the police chief and two officers entered the room.

"You will go to see the Deputy Attorney General."

"Who is the Deputy Attorney General, and what will he do with me?" I wondered. They proceeded to blindfold me. I was handcuffed to another police officer while being escorted to a vehicle. I was placed with four other policemen to guard me. The police chief was in the front seat next to the driver with a partition separating us. When the car started moving, they removed the mask and I was able to see the street. At this time, I realized that I had been arrested and was going to jail. I prayed in my heart asking the Lord Jesus Christ to stand by my side. I prayed that He would strengthen and support me by His Holy Spirit and help me to be a testimony to these police officers.

I felt very proud and honored because I was arrested for Jesus Christ. I felt a happiness and joy that I cannot describe. I started to understand what the apostle Paul meant in his words to Timothy, **"Remember that Jesus Christ, of the seed of David, was raised from the dead according to my gospel, for which I suffer trouble as an evildoer, even to the point of chains; but the word of God is not chained"** (2 Timothy 2:8-9). They put chains of steel on my hands, but they could not chain God's word in my heart and life! So I decided in my heart to speak boldly, trusting the Lord Jesus to stand by me and strengthen me.

Right then, my prayer was interrupted when one of the soldiers asked me, "Why did you get arrested?"

I answered him, **"Because I am a Muslim that has come to believe in Jesus Christ**."

All the officers were astonished at my statement. Then one of them asked, "Why would you do such a thing!?"

I started to tell them the story of my conversion to Christianity. The men listened intently to all I had to say. I shared about the love of God, who died for my sins, who came to save sinners, of which I am the first. It was as if I was talking to a group of Christian people, bold and unafraid. I was testifying to them with control and strength.

I continued talking until the police chief opened the window separating him from the rest of us. He was spewing the worst curse words at the officers because they were listening to my testimony. He ordered me to shut up and stop talking. Just then we reached the headquarters of the Deputy Attorney General.

Oh how much I thank my God for the book of Acts, which I had read before I was arrested. I had been praying that I could have the honor of suffering for my Lord. I was jealous of the believers I read about who went to jail because of Jesus. I was praying that the Lord would make me like them. This was a powerful preparation for what followed. I couldn't imagine what was going to happen to me. I was unaware of the torture, discrimination and pain that I was going to go through, but my eyes were on my Master and Lover, Jesus, who died for me, changed me and freed me.

Truly the Lord answered my prayer. I was arrested and put on trial because of the hope of the resurrection. I experienced the words of the apostle Peter, **"If you are reproached for the name of Christ, blessed are you, for the Spirit of glory and of God rests upon you. On their part He is blasphemed, but on your part He is glorified"** (1 Peter 4:14). And truly the Holy Spirit filled me throughout the upcoming interrogation.

## TESTIMONY BEFORE THE DEPUTY ATTORNEY GENERAL

Upon entering the security building I was taken to a second floor office, guarded by four armed police men. The officer I was handcuffed to released the handcuffs and showed me into the office. I was met by the Deputy Attorney General. A professional, sophisticated man in his thirties. He was sitting on his desk as he directed me to sit on a chair that was positioned directly in front of him. He introduced himself as Hisham Hammoudah and his first question to me was, "Why have you converted to Christianity?"

I began by telling him that I was born into an important Muslim family, well known in Egypt. Then I shared my story of conversion to Christianity and how I never intended to become a Christian. I explained how I went to church to make fun of the Christians. Then I told him how, quite unexpectedly, while reading The Lord's Prayer, I felt God's intense love for me.

I went on to tell him, "I awoke the next morning with a great desire to learn more about Jesus. I asked my friend Mamdouh for a Bible. I began reading the Bible immediately. That same morning I read through the Gospels of Matthew and Mark until Mamdouh told me it was time for lunch."

"At lunch I shared with Mamdouh about what had happened to me the previous night while I was reading The Lord's Prayer. That God came to me and announced that He was my Father. I shared with him what I read in the Bible about how Jesus fed the five thousand with two fish and five loaves of bread." This is a story which is familiar to Muslims because it is told in the Qur'an. "I shared with Mamdouh the many miracles that the gospels record Jesus doing such as healing the sick, casting out demons, and raising the dead.

I was drawn to this caring, sensitive, compassionate and powerful Jesus. As I made comparisons between Jesus and Muhammad, I was beginning to see how superior Jesus is to Muhammad. I was also beginning to realize how different the God of the Bible is from the Allah of the Qur'an."

"After Mamdouh and I finished lunch I went back and read the last two gospels. I read in the Gospel of John that Jesus performed so many miracles that, '...if they were written one by one, I suppose that even the world itself could not contain the books that would be written' (John 21:25). The more I read of Jesus, the more I became attracted to His personality. I was impressed by His honorable teachings, life and His powerful and encouraging miracles. I was falling in love with this person called Jesus. I could see that the Bible was not an unclean book because of the pure words of Jesus' teachings. I decided to go back to church because I wanted to learn more about the Bible. Each time I attended the church, I discovered more and more about the God of the Bible. I went often because I was hungry to learn the truth."

I explained to Mr. Hammoudah, "I began to understand that not only was God my heavenly Father, but He loves me even though He knows I am a sinner. The God of the Bible provided a way for me to be able to go to heaven, even though I am worthy of judgment. The Bible tells us that, '...God demonstrated His own love toward us, in that while we were still sinners, Christ died for us'" (Romans 5:8).

"God, who created me, loves me and made a way so that I wouldn't have to go to the place of suffering which awaits every sinner on judgment day. He did this by coming to the earth in the form of a human body, the body of Jesus Christ. He came to pay for our debts against Him. He sacrificed for all people by dying a shameful death on a cross. Jesus' death on the cross satisfied God's judgment against us so that we don't have to go to the place of torment!"

Mr. Hammoudah listened quietly while I poured out my heart. I was amazed how quickly I was recalling God's word. I knew God had prepared me for all that I would face and would inspire my words with His Holy Spirit.

I continued to tell Mr. Hammoudah that, "The Bible says, **'God has reconciled you by Christ's physical body through death to present you holy in His sight, without blemish and free from accusation'** (Colossians 1:22). He only asks that we believe and receive this wonderful salvation! The Bible also says, **'But as many as received Him, to them He gave the right to become children of God, to those who believe in His name'** (John1:12). And gladly, I received this amazing gift!"

I continued to explain, "God worked in my heart, removing all of the objections and prejudices I had against the truth. God showed me that He can do whatever He desires, however He chooses. This opened my heart to understand that God did become a man in the person of Jesus Christ."

"Both the Qur'an (Q4:164) and the Bible (Exodus 3:2) record God talking to Moses in the form of a burning bush. If God can come to Moses in the form of a burning bush, why would it be so difficult for Him to come in the form of a human? God is our creator and He can do anything! The Bible says, **'And without controversy great is the mystery of godliness: God was manifested in the flesh, Justified in the Spirit, Seen by angels, Preached among the Gentiles, Believed on in the world, Received up in glory'**" (1Timothy 3:16).

"I know this may be hard to understand and accept. Many Muslims consider this belief, of God becoming flesh, to be infidelity. I used to think this as well. But really, the infidelity is limiting God! If God is the Creator of everything that exists, His power and capabilities are unlimited. Isn't it blasphemy to limit God?"

## ANALOGY: THE PRESIDENT OF THE UNITED STATES

Let me ask you, is it possible for the President of the United States to leave the White House and visit the poor living in the slums of New York? What would you think if he did this? Spending time with them, shaking hands with them and listening to them? Would this lessen his status? Would this make him unable to continue conducting his other responsibilities as the President? And what do you think the reaction of the people of New York would be towards the President? Wouldn't they be very grateful that he took time out of his busy schedule to meet with them to learn how he could better help them? Wouldn't the fact that he left the comfort, security, and grandeur of the White House to spend time with them cause them to love and esteem Him even more?

God's coming to us is not infidelity. God's coming to us does not prevent Him from continuing to hold the universe together, for He can do anything. God's coming to us should not lessen our opinion of Him, but rather cause us to esteem Him even more because we can see that indeed our own Creator cares for us.

This is what God did for us. He came at just the right time in history to meet the poor and needy, to heal them of their diseases. The Bible says, "…**God anointed Jesus of Nazareth with the Holy Spirit and with power, who went about doing good and healing all who were oppressed by the devil, for God was with Him**" (Acts 10:38). The more we get to know Him, the more we love and appreciate Him because we see His beautiful character and learn more of His attributes. It is written about Christ that, "**He is the image of the invisible God, the firstborn over all creation**" (Colossians 1:15). If we want to know God and see Him, we only need to go to Jesus Christ.

> "And my speech and my preaching were not with persuasive words of human wisdom, but in demonstration of the Spirit and of power."
>
> 1 Corinthians 2:4

I learned much more about God through Jesus than I had ever learned about Him in Islam. The God of the Bible is very different from the god of Islam. We are taught in Islam that Allah is vengeful and deceitful (Q 3:54) (Q 13:42). That we are his servants and he is our master. We are afraid of him, as a slave is to his master. Our relationship with Allah in Islam is one of great fear.

The people of the Bible know God as their Father and loving Creator. We are His children, and as beloved children, we are always in His thoughts, and He delights in us! The Bible tells us that God **"having predestined us to adoption as sons by Jesus Christ to Himself, according to the good pleasure of His will"** (Ephesians 1:5). We are told that Jesus made the way for our salvation. **"In Him we have redemption through His blood, the forgiveness of sins, according to the riches of His grace"** (Ephesians 1:7). Jesus saved us from the curse of the law which separates us from God because of our sins. Jesus' death on the cross satisfied God's anger against us and now we can forever have fellowship with Him!

## THE FATHER AND THE TABLE

Allow me now to give you an example of how God helps us obey him and live holy lives.

I will use the example of two fathers. One will be a harsh, mean father and the other will be a good, loving father.

Let's pretend that there are two families who are moving furniture in their individual homes. There is a heavy table that needs to be moved to another room in both homes. The father in the first family tells his young son to move the table by himself into the next room. When he sees that his son is unable to move the table he becomes very angry with him and punishes him, even though he clearly knows that his son is not strong enough to move the table by himself.

The father in the second family already knows that his young son is not strong enough to move the table by himself. So he says to his son who is eager to help, "let's move this table together." They are successful in moving the table to the other room and this father praises his son for a job well done. This gave the son great confidence!

God gave me this example to show me that with His help I can accomplish His will. God, the good Father helps his children to live holy lives. Without His help it is impossible to please Him and He knows this. But because He loves us, He provides the help we need.

God is completely holy and pure. We are sinners. There is no way we can come into God's presence in our sinful state no matter how hard we try. Truly it would be an impossible burden to try to gain God's approval on our own. God knows very well that we cannot meet His holy standards without His help. That is why Jesus had to die for us. With Jesus' death on the cross, God's anger against sinners (of which we all are) is satisfied. Now, not only can we have everlasting life with Him, but He helps us to grow in holiness, so that we can accomplish His will as we become more like Him! Now we can say with the apostle John, **"For this is the love of God, that we keep His commandments. And His commandments are not burdensome"** (1 John 5:3).

This is why, after I met Christ, it became very easy for me to love God, respect Him and follow His commandments. Because the relationship that attaches me to God is the fatherly relationship, not the slave and master relationship. God is alive to help me with my burdens and strengthen me in my weaknesses. He is holding my right hand and will never leave me. Is there anything that the Creator cannot do? No! Is it too hard for God to change me, strengthen me and raise me above my weaknesses? Surely not, for He is Most Powerful! The change that comes to help us live according to His will comes from Him, not from ourselves. As it is written, **"Therefore, if anyone is in Christ, he is a new creation; old things have passed away; behold, all things have become new. Now all things are of God, who has reconciled us to Himself through Jesus Christ, and has given us the ministry of reconciliation"** (2 Corinthians 5:17-18). **"...His divine power has given to us all things that pertain to life and godliness, through the knowledge of Him who has called us by glory and virtue"** (2Peter 1:3).

*"Now when they bring you to the synagogues and magistrates and authorities, do not worry about how or what you should answer, or what you should say. For the Holy Spirit will teach you in that very hour what you ought to say."*

*Luke 12:11-12*

# 11

# Three Questions

After giving my conversion testimony to Mr. Hammoudah, which was followed by another hour of intense questioning, I raised my heart to God. I prayed that God would give me a word to reach the heart of this man. The Holy Spirit gave me the boldness to ask him three specific questions.

I posed the questions to Mr. Hammoudah this way. I said to him, "Mr. Hammoudah, please allow me to ask you three questions. If you can answer them for me, then I will return to being a Muslim. But if you are unable to answer them, then I would like you to seriously study the Bible for yourself to learn about Christianity." I was surprised that he agreed to my request. This was a miracle that he allowed me to question him. Now I became the investigator and he the suspect!

I lost no time and quickly posed the first question to him. "Mr. Hammoudah, can you tell me, **does Allah love you?**"

"Only Allah knows," he repied.

Then I asked him the second question, **"Where are you going after you die, are you going to heaven or to hell?"**

"Only Allah knows," he answered again.

So I asked him the final question, **"Is Allah, in Islam, able to change you?"**

**"Allah doesn't change people, they must change themselves,"** (Q 13:11) he replied.

I then said to him, **"Have you noticed, Mr. Hammoudah, that you cannot definitively answers these questions?** You do not know if Allah loves you or not. You do not know where you are going to spend eternity and you are not sure if Allah is able to change you?" I continued, "It seems that your Allah is far away from you and he doesn't care to participate in your life. If the situation is like this, then why do you follow him?"

He replied by asking me the same three questions I asked him! **"Well, do you know if your God loves you?"** he asked.

**"Not only does He love me, but He also died for my sake on the cross,"** I answered.

**"Where are you going to go when you die?"** he asked.

**"I am going to heaven,** and as a proof of this, I tell you that I am not afraid of what you will do to me," I said. "I know fully well that you are capable of ordering my execution. But I am confident that I will be with my loving Father in heaven forever."

Then he asked me the third question, **"Did Christ change your life?"**

**"Yes,"** I replied. **"Christ changed me and gave me a new heart and a new life**. He removed me from the power of darkness and brought me to His amazing light. He saved me from my evil habits, the cursing that I used to do and the impurity that I used to live in. I am a new person!"

He then inquired, **"What do you think of the Qur'an?"**

"The Qur'an, in my opinion, isn't worth a third of a penny because it is not from God," I replied. There was a secretary in the room recording our conversation and he asked if he should record what I had just said. He was told to record everything.

He was so distraught over my words that as he was writing he began repeating aloud, "Forgive us, oh great God. Forgive us, oh great God!"

Mr. Hammoudah continued, **"And what then do you think of Muhammad the prophet?"**

"Muhammad is not a prophet from God." I replied. "A prophet isn't a prophet just because he likes the title. Muhammad does not have any of the abilities or proofs of a prophet. Maybe at the most he was a social worker who helped relations between tribal Arabs in the Middle East, but he wasn't a prophet sent from God."

Again, the anguished recorder repeated his chant, this time with even greater fervency, "Oh great God, forgive us!"

The investigation took over three hours. It ended with these words of Mr. Hammoudah declaring, "You are accused of the following five charges: leaving the religion of Islam, bigotry to Islam, destroying the country's peace, inciting dissension between different religious communities and passing out flyers that promote disloyalty to the governor, president and country of Egypt.

When I heard the charges that were leveled against me, I did not fear, rather I was filled with God's peace and had boldness to counter them. I lost no time in giving a defense to these five charges as God's Holy Spirit enabled me.

To the charge that leaving Islam is an offense, I referred Mr. Hammoudah to the Qur'an's own words which state that, "There is no compulsion in religion" (Q 2:256). "It was true that I was born a Muslim, but this was not a choice. After reading both the Qur'an and the Bible I became aware of the differences between the two religions. Then I made a conscious choice to believe the Bible." I reminded Mr. Hammoudah that, "According to the Qur'an, Islam gives the people the freedom to choose to believe, or not believe." I asked him, "If this is the case, how can it be a crime to leave Islam?"

To the second charge that I am bigoted against Islam, I asked, "How in good conscience can I not share with my friends and family, what I know to be true? I have found the truth that God loves me and that Jesus is the way the truth and the life, and not just for me but for all who will believe. How can I not share my joy about God's marvelous salvation with others?" I asked him, "How is my sharing this joy racism?"

Third, to the charge that I am destroying Egypt's peace, I asked, "How is it possible that I am able to destroy the peace of a whole country." I assured Mr. Hammoudah that, "The peace of Egypt, and of the whole world, is in the hands of the Prince of Peace, and there is no real peace without Him. The Bible states that Jesus is the Prince of Peace. The Scripture declares that, **'For He Himself is our peace, who has made both one, and has broken down the middle wall of separation, having abolished in His flesh the enmity, that is, the law of commandments contained in ordinances, so as to create in Himself one new man from the two, thus making peace'** (Ephesians 2: 14-15). Christians are called to pursue peace, not enmity. **'Blessed are the peacemakers, for they shall be called sons of God'"** (Matthew 5:9).

To the fourth charge that I am inciting dissension amongst religious communities in Egypt, I answered, "In Christianity, unlike in Islam, there is no call for warring and jihad. In the Qur'an, jihad is accomplished by the sword, and the lowered status of those who are not Muslims, but this is not so in Christianity. In Christianity we are taught to love even our enemies. It is written, **'But I say to you, love your enemies, bless those who curse you, do good to those who hate you, and pray for those who spitefully use you and persecute you'** (Matthew 5:44). Christianity never calls for war, fighting, oppression, or coercion of others to persuade them to convert." I repeated to Mr. Hammoudah, "It is because of the overflow of joy in my heart that I share with others so that they can know this great joy and salvation as well." I stated that the accusation, of inciting one portion of the population to hate the other portion was, "unfounded and untrue."

Lastly, to the charge of passing out flyers that promote disloyalty to the country and its leaders, I responded, "The flyers I passed out have nothing whatsoever to do with the government, or rebellion. The flyers describe how one can know his Maker and become His child, just as I had. You should be glad, because I am helping others to know the true God who sacrificed His life for us so that we could have a relationship with Him forever. I sincerely hope God will stir your heart as well, to search for the way, the truth, and life."

The investigation ended with Mr. Hammoudah's signature on the document sealing the five charges against me. It stipulated that I was to be transferred to the Prison of Appeals, Eqypt's most notorious prison. I was handcuffed to one police officer on the right while a second police officer took hold of my left arm. I was then ushered out of the office to await my transfer.

The officers did not realize that, in fact, this was a great honor for me to be in chains for my Savior Jesus Christ. I felt honored and proud that God considered me worthy of testifying for Him before the Deputy Attorney General. As the apostle Paul declared, **"But by the grace of God I am what I am, and His grace toward me was not in vain; but I labored more abundantly than they all, yet not I, but the grace of God which was with me"** (1 Corinthians 15:10).

## THE HOLY SPIRIT SHALL SPEAK THROUGH YOU

In these four hours of being interrogated I experienced what Christ promised to those who follow Him. **"…When they bring you to the synagogues and magistrates and authorities, do not worry about how or what you should answer, or what you should say. For the Holy Spirit will teach you in that very hour what you ought to say"** (Luke 12:11-12).

I was a young man, only twenty three, when I was put before the magistrates and the powerful people in Egypt and I remember clearly, all these years later, how God spoke through me, teaching me in that very hour what I ought to say. I had no prior experience in the courts and had never been investigated, yet I was not afraid because I tangibly experienced God's Holy Spirit upon me during this time. Even now when I think of this, I am brought to my knees in gratitude, and thank my God for His grace and faithfulness to me. Indeed, Mr. Hammoudah, a man of prominence and experience was not able to give me an answer to the three questions I put forth to him. Jesus clearly was the victor in this investigation. Jesus promised his followers, **"…Lo, I am with you always, even to the end of the age"** (Matthew 28:20). Jesus too was with me in this hour. Praise God!

## THREE QUESTIONS TO MY READERS

Dear Reader, I ask you today the same three questions that I asked of Mr. Hammoudah:

"Does God love you?"

"Where are you going to go after you die?"

"Is your God able to change your life?"

If you, like Mr. Hammoudah cannot answer these three questions, I am urging you to find the truth before it is too late. Whether you are a Muslim or even a Christian by family name only, you need to find the answers to these questions. You will not find them in the Qur'an because the Qur'an is empty of God's love does not explain the way to heaven.

Ask yourself before you close your eyes and leave this life, are you going to heaven? If you answered that you are not going to heaven or that you do not know, then you need to search for the way that leads to eternal life. Jesus said of Himself, **"I am the way, the truth, and the life. No one comes to the Father except through Me"** (John 14:6).

The Qur'an and the prophet Muhammad guarantee you eternal hell. As he said, **"Not one of you but will pass over it (hell) this is, with thy Lord, a Decree which must be accomplished"** (Q 19:71). **In Arabic,** *wma menkom ela waredha* **means all Muslims must go to hell.** Even if you are doing good deeds, there is no guarantee of heaven in Islam. "Only Allah knows," as Mr. Hammoudah said. This is not the words of one who is confident that he will go to heaven.

This is the answer of Abu Bakr Al Sadiq the first successor of the prophet Muhammed, when he was asked the same question: "I don't trust the deception of Allah, even though if one of my feet was in heaven."[3] "Even the prophet Muhammad when Muslims asked him where he is going after he died he said: 'By Allah, though I am the Apostle of Allah, yet I do not know what Allah will do to me'" (Bukhari V.5 Hadith 266).

Finally, ask yourself, "Can Allah, in Islam, change you?" Mr. Hammoudah stated that only a person can change himself. Now how is this possible? How can a mere mortal, a weak human being, and a sinner by nature, change himself? It is impossible! That is why Jesus Christ came, to save sinners from the power of sin over them. Only God Himself can change us. As it is written, **"I have come that they may have life, and that they may have it more abundantly"** (John 10:10).

Make sure that of all the things you learn in this life, that you know the One who can truly save you. I tell you, truly I would not have been able to stand still in the presence of Mr. Hammoudah if it had not been God's Spirit giving me the boldness and presence of mind to testify before him. Just as the apostle Paul declared, "... **My speech and my preaching were not with persuasive words of human wisdom, but in demonstration of the Spirit and of Power"** (1 Corinthians 2:4). This was my experience as well.

*"...who are kept by the power of God through faith for salvation ready to be revealed in the last time."*

*1 Peter 1:5*

# 12

# The Prison of Appeals

Before I left Mr. Hammoudah's office, while he was finalizing my papers, I stated, "I would like to change the name on my government ID card to my new name, Daniel Abdel Massieh."

He said, "This is not possible because you were born a Muslim."

I reminded him again, "I did not choose Islam for myself, even the Qur'an states, 'There is no compulsion in religion.'"

He dismissed my concern and told me, "You are going to be transferred to the Prison of Appeals."

"How long am I going to be in prison?"

"You will be incarcerated for an *unspecified amount of time*," said Mr. Hammoudah.

Wondering what an unspecified amount of time meant, I inquired, "When will I have a court hearing?"

I was shocked when I heard Mr. Hammoudah say, "The prison you will be transferred to has no court. There is no course for readdressing your grievances."

## TO THE PRISON OF APPEALS

I arrived at the Prison of Appeals and was processed by a prison intake official. He asked me about my case and what I was charged with. I answered that **"I was a former Muslim, but now I believe in Christ."** He immediately insulted me and called in a loud voice for Ahmad the barber.

Ahmad the barber came in and began to shave my head. This was the way they humiliated the prisoners. I thought this was amusing and began to laugh. They began searching me for anything that resembled a weapon, but the only thing they found was the Bible that I carried in my pocket.

When the soldiers found the Bible they gave it to Ahmad, who asked me, "What is this book?"

"It is my Bible." I feared that he would take the Bible away from me. Ahmad and the soldiers flipped through the pages of the Bible, puzzled over it, and then gave it back to me. I was overjoyed that they allowed me to keep my Bible. I knew for certain that God was watching over me, orchestrating everything according to His good will.

Later I realized how much having the Bible was a miracle in sustaining me during my incarceration. Being isolated from believers, God's Word was my constant companion. I read the Bible morning and night. I felt the power of God's Holy Spirit upon me as I read about and meditated on the lives of the apostles who were also persecuted and jailed because of their belief in Jesus Christ. The Bible encouraged me greatly while I was in prison. I memorized many verses and wrote some of them on the walls of my jail cell. This period was one of preparation so that I could testify about Him. I experienced the keeping power of God. Just as the apostle Peter said, **"(We) are kept by the power of God through faith"** (1 Peter 1:5).

My dear Muslim,

Is God is calling you to come to Him with your burdens and your heavy sins, your evil habits and your sicknesses? He longs to carry these heavy burdens away for you and to heal you. You cannot do anything to remove these heavy burdens by yourself. You are his little child and He is your loving Father who misses you and wants to stand with you. Look to Him and wait for Him; talk to Him and call upon Him, for He is near. He answers the prayers of those who pray to Him. He desires to save you and free you from your chains. Come to Him and give Him the chance to prove how great a Father He can be to you, for He loves you very much.

*"But I say to you, love your enemies,
bless those who curse you, do good to those who hate
you, and pray for those who spitefully use you
and persecute you."*

*Matthew 5:44*

# 13

# Officer Jamal

Officer Jamal was famous throughout Egypt. He was regularly featured in Egyptian movies as the feared prison task master. He was a large, strong, muscled man with a thick mustache. His eyes were cold and steely like those of a hardened criminal, completely void of mercy. He wore the brown uniform of the prison guards fashioned with a whip at his side ready to be used. You would find him regularly insulting and intimidating the prisoners with cursing and foul language. He was lenient only to those who could provide him with a bribe. But officer Jamal wasn't only a movie actor, he was a real life prison official. And he was the man in charge of the prison inmates at the Prison of Appeals that I had just entered.

## COME IN INFIDEL

After my head was shaved by Ahmad the barber, I was taken to the second floor of the prison to officer Jamal. Officer Jamal seemed pleasant at first, and I didn't see him to be the dreaded man that I saw in the movies. He was very nice to me and assumed I was a political prisoner having committed a crime against President Sadat. He was certain I wasn't a criminal prisoner because of the clothes that I wore and the peaceful look on my face. After introductions, he asked why I was brought to the prison. When I told him that **I was a Muslim who now believed in Christ**, his face suddenly became contorted. His relaxed demeanor changed into one of a monster poised to attack his prey. Immediately and without notice, he lunged at me with his whip and began hitting me violently on my face, hands, legs and torso. None of the officers standing by did anything to stop him. He continued hitting me and cursing at me until he finally tired of the task.

When officer Jamal felt he had sufficiently humiliated me, he grabbed me and very forcefully took me into the cell that was to be my "home." He thrust me in with the words, "Enter you kafer (infidel)!" The cell was a grey concrete structure with a high barred window that was left open.

Because my cell window was open twenty-four hours a day and the prison was unclean there were many fleas in my cell. They started biting me all over my face, body and under my clothes. I started to itch a lot and tried to fight against the fleas but after a couple of hours I surrendered to them. The second day I complained to officer Jamal. He gave me a plastic bottle filled with gasoline and advised me to wash my cell floor and body with it because the fleas did not like the smell. I took the bottle and thanked him. I did exactly what he told me and killed many of the fleas, but I was dying from the smell of the gasoline. I was praying that God will protect me from the effects of the gasoline on my lungs and indeed He did. In spite of the fact that I was covered in gasoline, I survived that night and I fell into a deep sleep. I praise God I never received any skin diseases. This was the beginning of seeing God's

> "BECAUSE HE HAS SET his love upon Me, therefore I will deliver him; I will SET him on high, because HE HAS KNOWN My NAME."
>
> PSALM 91:14

hand protecting me. Later, I heard of many prisoners who became very sick in this prison. Some even died due to the conditions. But my God is a living God.

There was no furniture or bedding, not even a cover or a blanket, even though it was the month of December. The only amenity that was in this cold drab cell was a tin pail. Officer Jamal gestured that this pail was to be used as my toilet. I was informed that I would be allowed out of my cell only once a day, for five minutes, to clean the pail.

My daily meal was a bowl of lentil soup, and once in a while I was given a piece of stale cheese. After five months, my family still did not know where I was. The other prisoners were allowed to have their families visit them and many would bring gifts such as home-cooked meals, clothing, toiletries, etc. The other prisoners used the gifts their families brought to bribe officer Jamal so that he would give them extra privileges. The other prisoners were allowed out of their cells frequently to shower, exercise and visit the other prisoners. They were allowed blankets and more substantial meals. Even those who were incarcerated for plotting against the government were given basic human rights. But because I was a man who left Islam for Christ, I was deprived of all privileges.

## ISLAM AND CONDITIONAL FORGIVENESS

I was crying from the pain of the whipping and trying at the same time to take in the bleakness of my circumstances when I began to pray for officer Jamal. I was praying that God would forgive officer Jamal for hurting me and that God would save his soul. I couldn't believe myself, I was actually praying for the man who had just beaten me mercilessly and then cast me into this cold, foreboding cell.

Before I had become a Christian, I had a strong desire for revenge. If someone insulted me, I would insult him back ten times. If someone attacked me physically, I would return the blows with a vengeance. I never imagined the day would come when I would love and pray for those who hurt and persecuted me. This was the miracle of Christ changing my heart, filling it with His love, even for my enemies. Jesus said, "...**Love your enemies, bless those who curse you, do good to those who hate you, and pray for those who spitefully use you and persecute you**" (Matthew 5:44). This can only be done by the power of the Holy Spirit which He gives to those who believe in Him. Praise God, I experienced this miracle first hand!

The teaching of the Qur'an encourages "**eye for eye, tooth for tooth**" (Q 5:45). In Islam, forgiveness is conditional, fostering pride, arrogance, and dissention. There are two cases in Islam where forgiveness is allowed: first, in the case where the insulting person apologizes. Second, in the case where the enemy converts to Islam. If the person does not apologize or convert, then they can be mistreated with impunity.

This type of conditional forgiveness is like that offered by gangsters or street thugs. In reality, this is a type of blackmail intended to force the offending party into submission. This is not real forgiveness. Real forgiveness does not require payment or recompense of any kind to the offended party. This is perfect love, to forgive one's enemies without expecting anything in return from them.

> "**THEREFORE YOU SHALL BE PERFECT, JUST AS YOUR FATHER IN HEAVEN IS PERFECT.**"
> **MATTHEW 5:48**

True forgiveness can only be realized by perfect love. God came to us in the form of Jesus Christ to model perfect love for us. When Jesus was being crucified on the cross by His enemies He could have struck them with blindness or any other kind of plague for what they were doing. But Jesus acted in a way that was totally contrary to the way a normal human being would act. Instead of commanding a curse or a disaster to come upon them he said, "...**Father, forgive them, for they know not what they do**" (Luke 23:34).

God gave us real examples in the life of Jesus. He showed us how to forgive, so that we (along with the help of the Holy Spirit, given to all believers) can truly love others as He does. He calls us to become like Him. The world is full of those who deny God and insult

Him publicly, but He does not send upon them a curse. Instead He lets His sun rise upon them, and gives them His blessings in the hope that they too will come to Him, their heavenly Father. God calls believers to love their enemies so that, **"…You may be sons of your Father in heaven; for He makes His sun rise on the evil and on the good, and sends rain on the just and on the unjust"** (Matthew 5:45).

This kind of forgiveness is not found in any religion except in Christianity. I did not learn what real love was until I learned how to love my enemies as Christ did. My tears were not just for the pain of my beating and circumstances, but also for officer Jamal in the hope that God would meet him and change him into His disciple. To this day, I still pray for officer Jamal in the hope that I will see him as my brother in heaven.

*"But I want you to know, brethren, that the things which happened to me have actually turned out for the furtherance of the gospel, so that it has become evident to the whole palace guard, and to all the rest, that my chains are in Christ."*

*Philippians 1:12-13*

# 14

# Bishop Mohammed

The jail rules allowed all prisoners to leave their cells freely from morning to noon where they could enjoy various entertainments, showers and amenities. All prisoners were given this freedom except me. I was released from my cell for five minutes a day to use the bathroom and to empty and clean my pail.

## MY CELL BECOMES A NEWS STATION

The prisoners soon became aware of the one prisoner who was not allowed out of his cell. I became the topic of much conversation. It was rumored that I was a notorious criminal who was too dangerous to be let out to fraternize with the other prisoners. This intrigued the inmates who began to come to my cell, one by one, to ask me what crime I had committed. They would talk to me through the small opening in my cell door. Sometimes I would talk for hours with the various prisoners who came by to ask the reason for my incarceration. When I told them that **I was a Muslim who now believed in Jesus**, they were astounded. This led me to share my testimony with over five hundred prisoners. My cell became a good news station and my story spread to all corners of the prison compound. Many came to me more than once to hear the story of my conversion.

## AL ANBA MOHAMMED

When officer Jamal heard that I was becoming a celebrity of sorts, he gave me the name, "Al Anba Mohammed," which means "The Bishop (Christian) Mohammed." He gave me this name to mock and humiliate me. He thought this would cause me increased psychological distress in addition to the other punishments. But God turned what officer Jamal desired as a curse, into a blessing for His glory. Because of my treatment, many were drawn to come hear my story and learn the reason for the hope that was in me.

The name, Al Anba Mohammed, had a strong effect on the prisoners and increased their curiosity in me. One of the prisoners who came to talk to me was a man who was scheduled to be executed. He asked me to tell him the whole story of how I met Christ. I shared with him how I came to believe in Jesus and how He changed my heart and gave me eternal life. I felt the Holy Spirit revealing to me that he was open to the Lord so I gave him my Bible to read. It was the only Bible that I had, but I felt God urging me to let him borrow it to read for himself.

After two days he came back to my cell, clearly affected by what he had read in the Scriptures. With tears filling his eyes, he asked me what he needed to do to be saved. I encouraged him to pray and invite the Lord Jesus Christ to come into his heart and life. We prayed together, and afterwards a great calmness appeared on his face. He was filled with the peace of the Lord, knowing for certain that he had been delivered from all his sins and welcomed into the arms of his Heavenly Father. He thanked me profusely and left rejoicing. All this took place through the small opening in my cell door.

The news of his conversion spread throughout the prison. When officer Jamal found out, he became enraged. He entered my cell and whipped me until I collapsed, helpless on the floor. He threatened me, ordering me not to talk to the prisoners or even say the name of Jesus and then left my cell. But God continued to put it on my heart to pray for officer Jamal. I prayed often for him to be delivered from the rage in his soul and that he would come to know Jesus as his Savior.

## The Cell of the Communists

After five months, officer Jamal decided that my current solitary confinement and deprivations were not sufficient to cause me to return to Islam or to prevent me from sharing my beliefs with the other prisoners who came to the window in my cell door. So he had me moved to a new cell with three Egyptian communist men whom he thought would persuade me to leave Christianity.

Even though officer Jamal himself was Muslim, like the majority of his countrymen, he was hopeful that maybe these communist men would pull me away from my Christian beliefs. In his mind, the prospect of me becoming a communist was less of an insult to Islam than becoming a Christian. There is a saying in Arabic which goes like this, "The enemy of my enemy is my friend." This is the logic that officer Jamal used in transferring me.

When I came to the cell of the communists, I introduced myself to them and told them the reason for my incarceration. The leader of these communist prisoners was a man named Kamal. He said that he was born a nominal Christian and later embraced communism.

The men in this cell started talking with me about their beliefs. They told me that the religions of the world are the "opiate of the people," and that communism has a "greater call." This supposed greater call is the harmony and equalization of all people, where there are no more "rich" or "poor." Of course what they didn't emphasize is that this "equalization" is accomplished through force and coercion, a jihad of different sorts.

They tried to change my beliefs through many stories and examples. Their leader, Kamal, was calling me to leave Christianity to become a communist. But thank the Lord, God gave me the victory as I shared Christ with them. I shared my testimony with them, about The Lord's Prayer and how God visited me and then dramatically changed me, just as I had shared with Mr. Hammoudah and the others. We had many discussions about communism and Christianity, and the Word of God had a special power that caused them to listen to me very carefully.

## Don't Touch El Anba Mohammed

Their leader, Kamal, began to protect me from the trials I suffered. In a miraculous way, God used Kamal to defend me and grant me favor with officer Jamal. He would tell officer Jamal, "Don't touch El Anba Mohammed or hurt him from now on!" Kamal had a strong influence in the prison and especially with officer Jamal, as he used to supply him regularly with money and cigars in return for favors. He implored officer Jamal to give me free time like the rest of the prisoners were given. He also made sure I received a mattress and a blanket, which I had not been allowed to have previously. Because of Kamal's defense of me, I never again had a problem with officer Jamal.

Kamal also shared with me the gifts that he received from his family such as special canned delicacies and home-cooked food. When I saw that God gave me favor in the eyes of Kamal, I asked him if he knew of a way that I could get word to my family. It had been five months, and they did not know where I was and what had happened to me. Kamal asked me to provide him with my brother's name and phone number. He said he would send someone to tell my brother where I was.

*"No temptation has overtaken you except such as is common to man; but God is faithful, who will not allow you to be tempted beyond what you are able, but with the temptation will also make the way of escape, that you may be able to bear it."*

*1 Corinthians 10:13*

# 15

# The Letter Under the Soap

One day, while I was in the prison bathroom, there was someone standing next to me at the sink. When I looked up to see who it was I was greatly surprised to see a very dear friend! This precious godly man was the man whom I first met when I had gone to the church to mock the Christians.

After my conversion, "Habibi," a nickname I affectionately gave him, meaning "My beloved," became a father to me. He helped raise me in the Christian faith after my own family rejected me. Habibi did much to mentor me after I became a believer. He was the very first person who supported me. He taught me from the Bible and was a living example of Christian behavior and showed me how to apply God's Word in my life. When I would come to his office early in the morning I would find him in prayer and reading his Bible. He would lovingly ask me if I had done my devotional time and Bible reading for that day. He taught me how to pray for everything. Even before he would start his car engine, he would beseech God for His blessing. He was the earthly vessel that the Lord used to teach me about faith in Jesus and the pure Word of God. Habibi taught me how to humble myself, to be gentle like Christ, and to respect all people with the pure love of Christ. He showed me how to live a life filled with the love and presence of God. I never expected to see him standing right next to me in the prison bathroom!

I was floored that he was standing before me. I wanted to talk to him about many things, but he wisely cautioned me not to talk, hinting that the prison spies might be listening. He told me to come back to the bathroom again after a few minutes. When I returned to the bathroom, he handed me a bar of soap with a piece of paper hidden under it. I pretended to wash my hands while I removed the paper. I handed the soap back to him and thanked him.

I went to my cell and took out the paper from this loving elder. I sat happily while I read this letter from one of the dearest people I had ever known. The words in the letter said: "My dear son, be strong! God is with you, do not be afraid!" These words greatly encouraged me after many months of prison and loneliness. I never expected to see another believer in prison, let alone a believer who had meant so much to me. This was the greatest gift to me, seeing this precious man.

## LEARNING ABOUT CHRISTIANITY

I remember the very first encounter I had with Habibi at the church where I had gone to mock the Christians. At the end of the church meeting, while I was anxious to leave with my friend Mamdouh, I saw an elderly man approach us. Not knowing that this man would change my life forever.

At that first meeting in the church, Habibi had a big smile on his face. Though he did not know me, he gave me a big hug and greeted me with the words, "My dear friend." His words were tender when he spoke to me and I could tell that he was being genuine. He asked me my name and when I told him that it was Mohammed his attitude towards me did not change. He was sensitive to me and his words were full of love and patience. I felt something unusual in this man, especially when he hugged me. I was not able to explain it then, but later I realized that it was Christ's love overflowing through him that I was feeling.

I realized later that the love of Christ filled Habibi's heart to love all people whether Christian or Muslim. Habibi was an example to me of our Savior's feelings toward us. Oh, how our Savior longs to show His love to us!

Habibi invited me to his home where he said he had a Bible study. I thought to myself at the time, "Maybe if I go to his house I will see the Christians doing sinful acts. So I agreed to go."

I remember the first time I visited his house. I was wearing baggy worn out denim jeans and my hair was very long, like in the style of the sixties. I had a package of cigarettes tucked in my pocket. The door to his house was open when I arrived. I saw Habibi standing by the door holding his Bible and teaching from it. When he sensed that I was behind him he opened the door and invited me to come in.

I entered the meeting and found many people, young and old, sitting and listening intently. I took a seat and listened as he taught from the book of Genesis in the Bible. He was explaining the meanings of the names given to the twelve sons of Jacob.

After the Bible study many Christians came to introduce themselves to me and to welcome me to their fellowship. I remember one man whose face was shining like the sun and I could see the love of Jesus expressed in his face very clearly. I learned later that there were many Muslim converts at the meeting, but I did not know this at the time.

Wanting to be sociable, I took the pack of cigarettes out of my pocket and began offering them to my new acquaintances. With smiles on their faces they each politely said, "No, thank you." They reminded me of carefree children with no worries. They seemed so content. They were singing great songs of gladness and praise. It was shocking to me to see a gathering of this size where no one was a smoker and where everyone looked so happy, at peace and innocent.

This was a far cry from what I had expected Christians to act like.

Over the next several months, I visited many of my new friends in their homes. I ate with them and learned about them. Their lives were an open book and they were genuine, loving and holy people in both word and deed. I never witnessed them cussing or saw them behaving badly. They did not argue or try to hurt each other. I did not see them engaging in sinful behavior at all. I realized that they were not even remotely like what was depicted of Christians in the movies or on television.

Sadly, however, this is not true of all those who call themselves Christians. There are those whom I call "nominal" Christians who are Christians in name only. They have a heritage of Christianity, but have no real relationship with Christ. Their Christianity is either purely ritualistic or secular and devoid of true belief. These are the westerners we see represented in the movies and on television, but they are a far cry from true believing Christians.

The true Christians are those the Bible describes as **"born again"** and who have a relationship with Christ (John 3:3). The Bible says that, **"There is therefore now no condemnation to those who are in Christ Jesus, who do not walk according to the flesh, but according to the Spirit"** (Romans 8:1). They have accepted Christ into their hearts. They are surrendered to Him and He is their Lord. They have a relationship with God as their heavenly Father and they walk and live according to His ways because they want to please Him. They understand His holy Word from the Scriptures and reflect the holiness of God in their behavior. Habibi and the believers I met at his home and in the evangelical church are the real Christians.

Unfortunately, the majority of those who call themselves Christians are those who are nominal. This kind of Christian brings shame to the name of Christ. These Christians are not born again, but are spiritually dead like the rest of those who do not know God. The Bible calls them the **"children of wrath"** and they will not inherit the promises of God (Ephesians 2:3). They live for themselves and act according to the principles of this world. They conduct themselves based on their pride and selfish desires. They do not know Christ or understand their spiritual depravity.

I thank the Lord for Habibi and the true godly Christians who showed me how a person who calls himself a Christian should live and behave. They are the ones who are a true reflection of Christ and His love.

## TWO MISTAKES MUSLIMS MAKE

My dear Muslim friend, don't judge Christianity by the way nominal Christians live, but by the teaching and commands of the Bible for His followers. Have you read the Bible for yourself? How can you make a fair judgment regarding Christianity without reading its source, which is the Bible itself?

The first mistake that Muslims make is that they believe that the Bible is an unclean book. Many Muslims are afraid to even touch the Bible, thinking that it will make them unclean. I was one of them until I began reading a copy of the Bible for myself. I found out that the Bible is a holy book and whoever reads and obeys it will be cleansed from his sins. Even the Qur'an states, "It is He who sent down to thee (step by step), in truth, the book, **confirming what went before it, and He sent down the law (of Moses), and the Gospel (of Jesus)**" (Q 3:3). We see from this verse that the Bible has been revealed and sent by God as a guide and a light for all people.

Let me quote to you a passage which is an example of Christ's teachings in the Bible. I am praying that you will get yourself a copy of the Bible so that you will see the holiness of God in the gospels and through Christ's teachings.

"**For the grace of God that brings salvation has appeared to all men, teaching us that, denying ungodliness and worldly lusts, we should live soberly, righteously, and godly in this present age, looking for the blessed hope and glorious appearing of our great God and Savior Jesus Christ, who gave himself for us, that He might redeem us from every lawless deed and purify for Himself His own special people, zealous for good works. Speak these things, exhort, and rebuke with all authority, let no one despise you**" (Titus 2:11-15).

Dear reader, did you read this carefully and think through each verse? It is very clear to any honest person reading it that the Bible calls Christians to deny all ungodliness and to pursue a godly life. Christians are to purify themselves from all kinds of evil activities and do good works until Christ comes to take them to heaven. In another place the apostle Paul says, **"For God did not call us to uncleanness, but in holiness"** (1 Thessalonians 4:7).

I was deceived for a long time believing that Christianity is a religion of infidelity. I believed that the Bible was calling Christians to do scandalous things such as drink liquor, commit adultery and live in worldly pursuits. But I discovered the truth after I began reading the Bible for myself. I found, as the Qur'an says, that the Bible was sent by God (Q3:3).

Muslims often make the mistake of judging all Christianity by the behavior of the nominal Christians in the west, who are not the true followers of Jesus. This kind of so called "Christian" is what the Bible describes as far away from Christ and His teaching.

Muslims mistakenly believe that what they watch in American movies is taught in the Bible. They believe that the homosexuality, adultery, killing, ungodliness, drunkenness and worldly living displayed in these movies are permitted in the Bible. Muslims do not realize that what Hollywood produces is not true Christianity. Not in the least!

God says that the nominal Christians will be rejected by Christ at His second coming and in the day of judgment. The Bible clearly describes them and their end this way, **"For certain men have crept in unnoticed, who long ago were marked out for this condemnation, ungodly men, who turn the grace of our God into lewdness and deny the only Lord God and our Lord Jesus Christ"** (Jude 1:4).

As a Muslim I thought that the Christianity I saw from the nominal Christians was the only Christianity. Then I discovered the truth about Christ and His teachings touched my heart and my spirit. I witnessed His love and holiness from the real sources which are the Bible and the real Christians.

My Muslim friend, please get a copy of the Bible and start by reading the Lord Jesus' sermon on the mountain in the Gospel of Matthew, chapters five through eight. You will read for yourself the greatness of these words and see how holy the Bible is. The Qur'an states, "And Allah will teach Him (Jesus) the Book and wisdom, the law and the Gospel" (Q 3:48). Surat Al-Baqarah also states, "…We gave Jesus the son of Mary clear (signs) and strengthened him with the Holy Spirit" (Q2:87).

So do not be afraid to go to the source of Jesus' words, the Bible. If the Bible is God's holy Word, then you should find that it contains only truthfulness, nobleness, pureness, loveliness, justice and holiness in its pages. Those who are honest in their search will not be afraid to read it objectively.

## WITH THE TRIAL COMES A WAY OF ESCAPE

After our first meeting in the prison bathroom, Habibi and I began to meet regularly by the sink, passing notes to each other under the soap bar. Through the notes we passed to each other I became aware that others, like me, were also being jailed and experiencing persecution for their faith. I knew then that I was not alone in suffering this pain. The communication between us continued for many days *under the soap bar*, until my dear friend was transferred out of the Prison of Appeals.

Habibi's presence had greatly encouraged me. I knew that God had sent him so that we could be mutually encouraged. Christ knew the loneliness and pain I was suffering in the Prison of Appeals. He knew that I needed to be encouraged. Christ always knows what we need. He knew that I missed contact with other believers terribly and He sent me Habibi so that I could be refreshed and renewed. Through Habibi, Christ provided me with more than I ever thought possible. This is how our heavenly Father helps us in our weaknesses and trials, even in the middle of persecution.

My dear reader, if you are a believer and are going through hardship or persecution, or have left loved ones behind, be encouraged! The Lord Jesus Christ loves you and He is with you. He will make the way of escape so that you can bear the trial you are under. Do not be afraid. Stay strong and be patient!

*"What then shall we say to these things? If God is for us, who can be against us?"*

*Romans 8:31*

# 16

## The Beginning of Happiness

Kamal, the communist, came through on his promise to get word to my brother. There was someone he knew in prison who regularly sent messages to his family by throwing a stone with a note attached to it over the prison fence. His family would come by later to pick up the stones that he sent over. At Kamal's direction, he sent a note asking his family to get in contact with my older brother. The note included my brother's contact information and where my brother could find me.

When word reached my brother, he notified the rest of my family and called the Prison of Appeals. They were told that I was indeed at this jail and that I was incarcerated because I had changed from Islam to Christianity.

My brother succeeded in getting permission from the Egyptian Secret Service to visit me at the prison. The Egyptian Secret Service warned my brother not to help me or make it easy on me. They wanted to keep pressure on me to renounce my faith in Christ.

When my family came to visit me, our meeting was very emotional, filled with many tears. My father and older brother hugged me tight. My mother was crying and crying as she began to beg me to leave Christianity, "I love you so much and I cannot watch you suffer in this prison, please tell them what they want to hear so you can come home!"

I told her, "I love you so much, mother, and I appreciate your tears, but I cannot leave Christ. He changed me and promises to love me and keep me to the very end. He loved me so much that He died for me on the cross, so how can I leave Him?"

I recalled the words of Christ, **"He who loves his father or mother more than me is not worthy of Me"** (Matthew 10:37). My mother loved me in the natural way that a mother loves, but Jesus loves me in a deeper way, for all eternity. Christ accepted the humiliation and shame of the cross for me, to save me from eternal fire, **"...for the joy that was set before Him endured the cross, despising the shame, and has sat down at the right hand of the throne of God"** (Hebrews 12:2). The Lord Jesus told his disciples, **"Greater love has no one than this, than to lay down one's life for his friends"** (John 15:13).

My mother pleaded, "You can let the love of Christ be in your heart, but keep your beliefs to yourself and don't tell anyone about it."

"Mother, I cannot deny Christ. He died for me and changed my life." When she saw that there was no use in talking to me, she tried to get me to change my mind by giving me a lot of good food and showing me affection.

My older brother said, "Oh Hamada (the nickname he would call me), we are in a Muslim country that believes in the sword. So when you see the sword coming to cut off your head, shouldn't you duck so that you won't be killed by it? Where are all those Christian people you used to pray with in the churches? They did not come to rescue you or help you in this jail. They all left you, to be beaten and insulted and to suffer alone, worrying instead about their own lives…. why?"

While I listened to my brother, I remembered the words of Paul the apostle to Timothy, **"At my first defense no one stood with me, but all forsook me. May it not be charged against them. But the Lord stood with me and strengthened me, so that the message might be preached fully through me, and that all the Gentiles might hear. Also, I was delivered out of the mouth of the lion"** (2 Timothy 4:16-17).

"Yes, what you are saying is true, everyone got scared and forsook me. Thank God He has never left me. Not for one minute! He didn't leave me when I faced Mr. Hammoudah, Ahmad the barber, Kamal the communist, officer Jamal, or in the other deprivations I suffered in the jail. God has been with me to help me and strengthen me through all these trials and difficulties."

"It was through the pain of these hard times that I experienced the trustworthiness of the Lord. I felt the Lord's beautiful hand always by my side supporting me, strengthening me and keeping me from danger. This is what the Scripture means by stating, **'…If God is for us, who can be against us?'"** (Romans 8:31) I continued.

I was so grateful to finally have my family in front of me, I needed them to understand my heart. I told them, "God allowed me to go through these pains so that I could taste a little of what He suffered for the whole world. What is my earthly suffering compared to the sufferings of the Lord Jesus Christ for my sins and the sins of the whole world? Christians can be hopeful in their sufferings because as the apostle Paul declares, **'…the sufferings of this present time are not worthy to be compared with the glory which shall be revealed in us'** (Romans 8:18). Christ has prepared for us His glories! Again the apostle Paul declares, **'…Eye has not seen, not ear heard, nor have entered into the heart of man, the things which God has prepared for those who love Him'** (1 Corinthians 2:9). I consider the sufferings I experienced for the sake of my Savior a great honor, and I cannot wait for the "glories" to come!"

After awhile, my brother saw that there was no use in preaching to me. He became angry and said, "You are being stupid! You are crazy for exposing yourself, and the whole family, to danger because of your belief in Christ!"

I remembered the words of the apostle Paul when he said **"For if we are beside ourselves, it is for God; or if we are of sound mind, it is for you"** (2 Corinthians 5:13). I answered him by saying, "My brother, I am here in jail for the crime of knowing God. Is this a crime that deserves death or jail? I have not been convicted of drug possession, theft or killing. What is the great crime that I have committed? What is my fault? Don't you remember how, before I became a Christian, I used to live for sin and worldly pleasure? But now I am a new person whom Jesus has changed and renewed and made a new creation."

Then to my surprise, my mother interjected, "I wish that your crime was drug possession! That would be easier on me than you becoming a Christian."

I wondered greatly of this great darkness that fills the Muslim heart. The Muslim who is a drug dealer or who lives in sin is considered much better than a Muslim whose life has been transformed by the power of Christ. I glorified Christ greatly because He had opened my eyes and set me free from this dark veil that covers the Muslim heart. Christ said, **"…I am the light of the world. He who follows Me shall not walk in darkness, but have the light of life"** (John 8:12). Hallelujah, how great is the light that Christ gives!

Then my brother asked me a strange question, "What did you tell Mr. Hammoudah during your investigation?"

I told him, "I shared my testimony about how I became a Christian."

My brother revealed to me, "I spoke at length with Mr. Hammoudah. He told me that he had investigated many Muslims who had converted to Christianity, and that even the Pope of Egypt (Baba Shanoudah), who had been investigated, never dared to say the things that you had said about Muhammad and the Qur'an. Mr. Hammoudah said that he was ready to let all these other Christians go free, but not you, because you had become a Christian for real."

I praise God that I was able to boldly testify to Mr. Hammoudah. I had no regrets regarding what I shared with him. I had no idea that I was going to be able to share with him so honestly and forthrightly. I was just a young, inexperienced man during this interrogation.

It was God who strengthened me and gave me the courage and boldness to speak without hesitation. I was not afraid of the lion's mouth, because God strengthened me, giving me courage and purpose of heart. Glory to His Name!

> "THE LORD is my light and my salvation; whom shall I fear? THE LORD is the strength of my life; of whom shall I be afraid? WHEN THE wicked CAME AGAINST ME TO EAT UP my flesh, my enemies and foes, they stumbled and fell."
>
> Psalms 27:1-2

In the logic of human understanding what my brother said was understandable, because he does not have the sweet experience of knowing Christ. But for me the presence of God with me is enough. Without Christ, even if I had the praise and adulation of the whole world, I would be nothing.

My father was quiet at our first meeting in the jail because of an unusual dream he had before my incarceration. In the dream Christ appeared to my father and told him not to persecute me. He told my father that I was walking in the right path. He also told my father to change his own name to that of "Micah." After the dream, my father came to me and asked me if there was anyone mentioned in the Bible with the name of Micah. I told him yes, that Micah was a prophet of God. Then he told me of the strange and captivating dream. With tears he asked me, "What should I do now, to become a Christian?" I told him to pray with me, to ask the Lord Jesus to forgive his sins, and to come live in his heart. Between sobs my earthly father prayed with me to accept Jesus as his Savior and Lord. Praise be to God!

At the close of our meeting, I hugged them all, and then was taken back to my cell. When I returned Kamal asked me, "What happened during your meeting in the visitor's room."

I told him, "My mother kept crying and begging me to return to Islam. I explained to her that I could not deny my Savior and Lord."

Kamal stated, "I am surprised that you were not shaken by your family's visit and your mother's pleading. I am amazed that you are willing to suffer for the name of Christ. This is not the type of Christianity that I am used to." This helped me to explain more to Kamal about the great love of Christ.

## God is Not in Debt to Anyone

I saw the hand of God turning all things for good. Officer Jamal thought that if he put me in the cell with the communists, that I would become one of them. Days and months went by and still officer Jamal did not see me becoming a communist or leaving Christ. Rather, the opposite happened!

Later, after our release from prison, Kamal the communist met up with my dear friend Habibi. Habibi shared at length with him about Christ and faith in the Lord. Kamal then became a real believer in Christ who knows, loves and enjoys his Savior. He is no longer a communist or just a nominal Christian, but a Christian for real!

God does not stay in debt to anyone. Kamal helped me inside the jail, and then the Lord met him outside the jail. Kamal was good to me, a follower of Christ. The Lord, in return, was good to Kamal, leading him to an abiding faith. Kamal became a new person in Christ and left the communists. Hallelujah! It happened as the Bible says, "So shall My Word be that goes forth from My mouth; It shall not return to Me void, but it shall accomplish what I please, and it shall prosper in the thing for which I sent it" (Isaiah 55:11).

> **"For I could wish that I myself were accursed from Christ for my brethren, my countrymen according to the flesh..."**
>
> **Romans 9:3**

## Miracles Inside the Prison

While in prison I was never allowed to shower, or to wash

with water. I had no toothbrush or toothpaste with which to brush my teeth. When my family finally came the prison officials would not let them bring me any kind of basic necessities. They deprived me in order to pressure me into recanting my belief in Christ. But thanks be to God who strengthened me and saved me from the mouth of the lion. In spite of the extreme circumstances, I never once became sick. I never had a skin disease, a cold or flu, a stomach problem, tooth or mouth problems, or any other kind of ailment which could have worn me down.

After my release a dentist friend of mine offered to look at my teeth. He expected to find a mouth full of bacteria, cavities, and gum disease, since he knew that I had no access to any kind of mouth hygiene while in prison. He was astonished to find that, in fact, I had no deleterious bacteria in my mouth and that I didn't need any treatment! He said that normally someone who was deprived of mouth hygiene for eight months should have had a mouth full of bacteria and germs, causing cavities and gum problems. Then, several months later, after regularly brushing my teeth, I went to see him again for a check up. Ironically, this time, he found a lot of bacteria present in my mouth which required treatment to eliminate. I knew then that God has power over everything, even the bacteria in my mouth! Glory be to God!

*"'No weapon formed against you shall prosper, and every tongue which rises against you in judgment you shall condemn. This is the heritage of the servants of the LORD, and their righteousness is from Me,' says the LORD."*

*Isaiah 54:17*

# 17

# What He Opens No One Can Shut

For eight months the authorities tried unsuccessfully to get me to deny my beliefs in Christ through physical and psychological pressure. I had been beaten three times with a whip, everywhere on my body and face. I was put in solitary confinement, no hot water, no shower, no shaving, no tooth brushing and no change of underwear. My toilet was a large can with sharp edges I would use my shoes to sit on so that I would not get cut. The rooms were infested with insects. I only had one meal a day that was brought out on a rug that they drug through the prisons and had everyone pick from it. I would often save some bread to use as a pillow.

During that time the Lord gave me great opportunity to share my faith with those in the prison. This created additional frustration for Mr. Hammoudah. I was not allowed contact with my family or loved ones. But in spite of this God, with great tenderness, took care of all of my needs. He showed me that He had not abandoned me. Just as God took care of the prophet Elijah when he fled from the evil King Ahab by feeding him with food brought by the ravens (1Kings 17:2-4), God took care of me through giving me favor with Kamal, the leader of the communists. He also brought me my dear spiritual father, Habibi. How great is our living God! He does not abandon those who love Him. As it is written, **"He is the Rock, His work is perfect; For all His ways are justice, A God of truth and without injustice; Righteous and upright is He"** (Deuteronomy 32:4).

## OUT ON BAIL

I remember one day when my brother came to visit me. He came to visit me often. We enjoyed a very close relationship, especially during this hard time. My brother explained to me how he had spoken to Mr. Hammoudah concerning my imprisonment. His position as a judge was beneficial with Mr. Hammoudah. He told me that he was able to arrange for my released on bail. He cautioned me that my release was contingent upon many conditions. My brother was told by Mr. Hammoudah that I was not allowed to evangelize, attend church or go to Christian meetings. If I disobeyed these stipulations Mr. Hammoudah said that my punishment would be worse than my present incarceration and that according to the Islamic Sharia law, "My blood would be spilled." If another Muslim were to kill me for any reason, the government would excuse him and he would not be arrested or punished. I am consider a traitor to Islam, deserving to be killed.

What a corrupt and strange religion that allows the killing and spilling of blood so easily! Islam stands on a foundation built on threats, killings and the sword. You are only safe if you submit to Islam. But what about the verse in the Qur'an that states, "There is no compulsion in religion?" I can relate with Aisha (Muhammad's youngest wife) when she said, "I wonder (greatly) about the Allah that grants Muhammad as he wishes."[4]

I left jail with the help of my brother in August of 1982. In the second day after I was released, I went to see Habibi, my spiritual father, who had been released several months earlier. I was so happy to be reunited with him and the people that I loved. I was not afraid of the threats against me. God allowed me to go through the circumstances I had just experienced and I knew that He would sustain me through whatever was before me. I knew that even if I were killed for my faith that it would be worth the price. I resumed going to church and meeting with my Christian friends. I also continued to proclaim Christ as I did before, but now I was careful to make sure that no one was spying on me or following me.

While in prison, I had learned how to avoid the surveillance of spies. This was one of the benefits of talking with the other prisoners. They told me how to know if I was being followed and gave me various tips on how to lose a spy. I used to jump and change taxis and busses many times to make sure that I wasn't being followed by anyone hired by the government. At times I would leave my house very early in the morning before the sun rose and then not come home again until after dark. This way no one could follow me or see me going to meetings. I knew the consequences that would happen to me if they caught me, but I was more concerned with the consequences for those who didn't know the Lord.

*"Unless the **LORD** builds the house, They labor in vain who build it; unless the **LORD** guards the city, the watchman stays awake in vain."*

*Psalm 127:1*

# 18

# A Dream Becomes Reality

## THE SALVATION OF MY MOTHER

After my release, I shared the Bible with my mother. I talked with her about the beauty of Christ and His holiness. I contrasted Christ's holiness and beauty with Muhammad's depravity. I explained to her the differences between the heaven of Islam and the heaven of Christianity. I also shared with her the miracles of Christ and His incredible sacrifice for humanity. I told her that because of our fallen nature, we are dead in our trespasses and sins, and that we are corrupted and rotten with no hope for heaven without Christ's sacrifice. I gave her the analogy of a clay vase. I told her how the vase became cracked and had no use for anything except to be thrown in the trash heap. But that God in His love, made a way for us to be reconciled and repaired. As God told Jeremiah the prophet, "… **Look, as the clay is in the potter's hand, so are you in My hand, O house of Israel!"** (Jeremiah 18:6). For God is able to shape us again into something that is beautiful in His eyes. When we put ourselves in His hands, His skilled fingers are powerful to raise us from the grave of our sins and clear the stain of our guilt. His compassion takes us from the power of darkness into the kingdom of His love.

My mother agreed with me that Christ's actions were greater than that of Muhammad's. She realized that, especially regarding Muhammad's many wives and his treatment of women, Muhammad's actions bore the stain of sin and spread the rotting stench of debauchery and evil. I reminded my mom what Aisha said, "Whenever Allah's Apostle wanted to fondle anyone of us during her periods (menses), he used to order her to put on an Izar (dress) and start fondling her." Aisha added, "None of you could control his sexual desires as the Prophet could."[5] Even though my mother did not openly express her faith in Christ, I know she believed in her heart. My mother feared Islamic law and never publicly confessed her belief in Christ.

After my mother passed away I was deeply sorrowful and wept a lot over her death. But God gave me a strange dream about her. The dream was more realistic than other dreams that I have had. I believe that through this dream, God was telling me that my mother was with Him in heaven.

I dreamt that my mother's house was on fire. The fire blazed all through the house, consuming everything in its path. I was very disturbed by this fire and its devastation. Suddenly, I heard someone knocking on the door of my home. When I stood to open the door, I was very surprised to see my mother standing there. I said to my mother, "I heard your house had burned in the fire!"

She replied saying, "Yes my son, the house burned but I was saved out of it."

I was very consoled by this dream. It confirmed to me that my mother had accepted Jesus Christ into her heart and that Christ's blood saved her so that she now was safely in heaven. I greatly look forward to the day I will see her in the beauty and expanse of heaven.

## SAMIA

Soon after my release from prison, I prayed diligently that God would lead me to a godly Christian woman to be my wife and helper in this life. Then one night, I had an unusual dream. In this dream, I found myself at the home of one of the families that attended a certain church where I had worshipped and given my testimony.

I had casually known this family from before my time in prison, but I had never thought about marrying any of their daughters. In the dream I saw myself talking with the father of the house, asking him for his permission to marry his daughter, Samia. Though I recognized Samia from the church where I had given my testimony, I had never thought about marrying her. So even to me this came as a surprise!

In the dream, the father became enraged at my request. He told me in no uncertain terms that he was refusing my request. Then with authority I rose up, and pointing to him directly with my right hand stating, "I came with the authority and in the name of the Lord Jesus Christ!" At this, the father's face and composure changed. His expression became calm, and then I awoke.

After the dream, I was certain that God had answered my prayer for a godly wife. I contemplated how I was going to go to the home of this Christian family to ask for permission to propose to Samia. When I remembered the way her father reacted in my dream, I became anxious. I kept seeing her father's vexed face before me, but then God reminded me how the dream had ended. I was encouraged when I remembered the authority the name of Jesus had, and the power it issued to disarm her father.

I did not tell Samia a word about my dream. I decided, instead, to approach her mother who was respected in the church for being a devout and righteous woman. Her love for the Lord was apparent in her service to others. She was a mature Christian whom the Lord had also appeared to in multiple dreams and visions. I felt that this godly woman would listen to me and consider the dream I'd had.

I went to her house and told her mother about my dream and my intentions to propose to her daughter. After listening to me carefully, her mother gave me her approval, but she could not hide her anxiety. She expressed to me her concerns regarding her husband, and how he would react to the idea of their daughter marrying a former Muslim, especially one whose name is "Mohammed." In Muslim countries, it is considered shameful for someone from a Christian family to marry someone from a Muslim family under any circumstances. Samia's father was not a true believer in Christ at the time, but a Christian in name only. He would not have the same sympathies that his wife did to my dream. Even though he had heard my testimony, he did not really understand the power of Christ to change someone like me.

Her mother asked me, "What shall I say to my husband after you talk to him?"

I told her to say to him, "If this is from God, no one can stand against it." With these words, I left their home to return later to talk to her husband.

I prayed fervently for God to stand by me in this matter. Again I went to Samia's house, this time to talk to her father to ask permission to propose to his daughter. Sure enough, just as I had seen in the dream, he reacted to me with those angry eyes at the audacity of my request.

He said to me, "Tell me, Mohammed, if my daughter were to marry you, what would your children call their uncle?" Since my brother's name is Mostaffa, he was making a sarcastic joke about the impossibility of such a union. He continued to make fun of me because I was from a Muslim root. Even though I felt hurt and humiliated by his insults, I prayed silently for God to give me wisdom in how to answer him.

Then, as I had in the dream, I began speaking with authority. I defended my situation by tell him, "I did not chose to come from a Muslim root. When I met the Lord Jesus Christ, I accepted Him as my personal Savior. And you know the honesty of my testimony in Christ. I promise you, that I will take care of your daughter. No harm will come to her." I continued, "Now let me ask you a two choice question: Would you rather your daughter marry a convert by the name of Mohammed who promises to take care of her and love her as he loves himself, or would you rather her marry a 'Christian' guy by the name of George, who won't take care of her and may divorce her later in life?"

With these words he suddenly became calm and thoughtful, just as he had in my dream! Then he said to me, "Your words are convincing, but it is not only up to you. We must ask Samia what she wants." He said that he would ask Samia what her wishes were and let me know the outcome the following Sunday.

I couldn't believe what had just happened. Everything that I saw in the dream was fulfilled, confirming to me that indeed this girl was the one who God intended for me to marry. I had only seen Samia maybe three or four times and I had never really talked to her. I began to wonder what she would think of this proposal of marriage, since she hardly knew me. But I left this for God to work out. As God prepared Eve for Adam, I believed that God would prepare Samia's heart for me.

The following Sunday came. I went, as planned, to meet her father at their house. I was very anxious to hear how she responded. I met her father at the door and he had a sad expression on his face. I was not sure what to make of this. Then he told me that to his great surprise, she had accepted my

> "Do not fear the reproach of men, nor be afraid of their insults."
>
> Isaiah 51:7

proposal! Her father never imagined that she would agree to marry me since she hardly knew me. Joy filled my heart when I heard this marvelous news. I rejoiced along with Samia and her mother and indeed, we were engaged that very day in 1982!

As Samia and I began our courtship, I asked her why she agreed to marry me. She told me that when her father first told her of my proposal of marriage that she was very concerned because she knew this would bring sharp disapproval from the community. Women from Christian families do not marry men from Muslim backgrounds, even if they do become believers. She knew that by agreeing to become engaged to me, there would be many hardships. These were serious concerns with no clear answers. Her mother had told her of the dream that I had. She knew that I, as well as her mother, felt strongly that this dream was from God, but she needed God to confirm this to her as well.

Samia spent much time that week praying and reading God's Word. She asked God to give her wisdom from the Holy Scriptures. Samia received no clear direction until the following Sunday. The very day she was to give her answer regarding my proposal. Early that morning, Samia was reading in the book of Isaiah when God's Word suddenly came alive to her, **"Listen to Me, you who know righteousness, you people in whose heart is My law: Do not fear the reproach of men, nor be afraid of their insults. For the moth will eat them up like a garment, and the worm will eat them like wool; but My righteousness will stand forever, and My salvation from generation to generation"** (Isaiah 51:7-8).

Further confirmation came as she sat in church that morning listening to the sermon. The sermon was on the Virgin Mary's encounter with the angel who had announced to her that she was to be with child. The pastor discussed how Mary was concerned about this and asked the angel, **"How can this be, since I do not know a man?"** (Luke1:34). The pastor surmised that Mary wondered what others would think since she was not yet a married woman. When Mary asked the angel how she could have a child since she was a virgin the angel told her that the Holy Spirit would come upon her to cause her to conceive. She responded with great faith declaring, **"… Behold, the maidservant of the Lord! Let it be to me according to your word!"** (Luke 1:38). When she heard the pastor speak the words of Mary, Samia felt God's Spirit piercing her heart. She was convinced that God had confirmed to her that the marriage should take place. Samia said that she, like Mary, had no choice but to also say, "Behold the maidservant of the Lord! Let it be to me according to your Word!"

## THE HAND

Samia realized that she would have to ignore the threats, insults and hardships that were sure to come, and come they did.

About a month after our engagement, I became exasperated with the insults that were constantly leveled at me from Samia's father. I did not know how I could endure life with a father-in-law who demeaned me relentlessly. One day he was so rude to me that I hastily announced to him that I was breaking off the engagement. I handed him the engagement ring and left the house.

The next day Samia's father called me on the phone saying that he urgently needed to see me. I went to meet him at his work place. When I saw him I was shocked to find that his face was bruised and swollen, like he had been in a bad fist fight and had been severely beaten up. I asked him what happened.

He explained to me that the morning after I handed him the engagement ring, he was in his bathroom getting ready for work. Suddenly, out of nowhere, he saw a human hand appear in the air that began slapping, hitting, punching and throwing him all over the bathroom. The hand slammed him into the bathroom wall over and over and wouldn't let up. He said he was screaming loudly for help but no one was able to open the bathroom door to rescue him. This continued for several minutes, and then, just as suddenly as it had appeared, the hand disappeared. Samia's father hurriedly opened the bathroom door and ran outside, terrified by what had just happened. He said he was convinced that this was from God to chastise him for the way he had been treating me. After telling me what had happened to him, he apologized profusely. He hugged me hard and humbly asked me for my forgiveness. While still clinging to me, he implored me to set a date for the marriage. I assured him of my forgiveness and then I told him that I would like to set the date for the following month. He agreed immediately, so the date was set.

I was so happy we would be married soon. I was unaware, however, of a plot to sabotage our wedding. Samia's uncle (her mother's brother) had hoped Samia would be his son's future wife. When he found out that she was betrothed to me he planned to stop the wedding. He decided to notify the police to ensure that the marriage would be canceled. The same day that he was on his way to the authorities he stopped first at a local restaurant to have lunch. Immediately after the meal he became deathly ill with food poisoning and had to be transported to the hospital. While in the hospital he confessed to his family that he was on his way to the police station to have the marriage stopped. He asked Samia's mother to send for me so that I would forgive him and pray for him to be healed. So I came to the hospital and I forgave him from my heart and asked the Lord to touch him and heal him. The uncle recovered and there were no further oppositions to the marriage. I praised God that even while I was unaware of those who were working to destroy our engagement and marriage He was behind the scenes defending me!

Samia and I were married December 19, 1982, exactly one year to the day of my incarceration. The marriage occurred in a church in Egypt called "Al Ma'aide." This was another victory of Jesus Christ in my life and proof to all those around me that God's plans cannot be thwarted when we are following Him. I experienced what the prophet Zachariah said, "...**Not by might nor by power, but by My Spirit says the LORD of Hosts**" (Zechariah 4:6). I knew indeed the truthfulness of God's promises to His children. As the Psalmist said, "**They looked to Him and were radiant, and their faces were not ashamed**" (Psalm 34:5). God's promises to His children are not empty words, but they are the power of God to establish His will in our lives.

My advice to everyone who is searching for their spouse is to take this testimony to heart. Seek God diligently and wait patiently. He will lead you to your soul mate. Do not be seduced by human wisdom or fall for attraction. "**In all your ways acknowledge Him, and He shall direct your paths**" (Proverbs 3:6). Trust your heavenly Father. He knows what you need even before you ask Him (Psalm 139:4). He is rich and generous and He delights in blessing you. "**...Unless the Lord builds the house, they labor in vain**" (Psalm 127:1). May God bless you as you build your house on the eternal Rock!

In March of 1983, Samia, and I moved to Spain as missionaries. We were in charge of all the correspondence to Muslims in North Africa. There was a outreach program offered to Muslims through the mail called "Allah Akbar." I was in charge of responding to their letters and answering their questions. When we noticed that someone was getting close to accepting Christ we would cross the border to Morocco to meet with them. We would pray with them, teach them the Bible and train the new believer to start a small underground church. We met with many Muslims who gave their life to Christ. We would also smuggle Bibles across the border and go to Morocco and pass them out in the street. One day we got stopped by a Moroccan soldier. I had over 500 Bibles in my trunk. He asked me where I was from and I told him that I was from Egypt. He was excited that he met an Egyptian because Egyptian people are considered witty and he asked me to tell him a joke. I prayed for a joke to distract him. I told him a joke and He laughed and asked the other soldiers to open the gates for me. I passed through without them searching my vehicle. If they had searched my trunk that day I would have been arrested.

During this time, Samia became pregnant with our first child, a son. We were concerned about delivering him in Spain because his name would be recorded under my Muslim name, Mohammed Kamel. We knew if he visited any Middle Eastern country, especially Egypt, he could get into a lot of trouble with that name. When a pastor in Michigan invited me to be his assistant in March of 1984, we knew it was from the Lord. He had read of my testimony in the newspaper and wanted to help us flee from the dangerous conditions we lived in, and knew that we could be a great benefit to his church.

We knew that God's plan was for us to come to the United States so we could raise our children in the land of freedom. We praised God for his perfect timing and our son Joshua was born in Michigan as a citizen of the United States. During this time, I assisted the Arabic pastor in visitations, leading small group Bible studies, home prayer meetings and preaching the word on Sunday. I would hold many Bible studies and train Christian Arabs how to share their faith effectively with others.

Because of the cold weather and extreme temperature adjustment from moving to Michigan I came down with pneumonia and my health was growing worse. My wife and I were praying for God to show us His plan. It seemed very hard to live in Michigan because we were used to the dry, desert weather of Egypt. One evening the phone rang. I answered the phone and heard a familiar

Egyptian voice saying, "Hi Daniel, are you here in the states and I didn't know? I am your friend E. T." He was a pastor in Egypt and was now living in California. He told me he heard about the work I was doing in Michigan and asked if I would like to move to California and help his ministry. He mentioned that he was praying for someone like me to come and help him in his new church he planted among Arabic speaking people at Costa Mesa Calvary Chapel.

My wife and I prayed about this new opportunity and the Lord confirmed our move to California. In March of 1985, the three of us moved to California. I performed many of the same duties here as I did in Michigan. I knew that God was training and preparing me. I knew He had a great plan for us.

"Now it happened, the day after, that He went into a city called Nain; and many of His disciples went with Him, and a large crowd. And when He came near the gate of the city, behold, a dead man was being carried out, the only son of his mother; and she was a widow. And a large crowd from the city was with her. When the Lord saw her, He had compassion on her and said to her, 'Do not weep.' Then He came and touched the open coffin, and those who carried him stood still. And He said, 'Young man, I say to you, arise.' So he who was dead sat up and began to speak. And He presented him to his mother."

Luke 7:11-15

# 19

## The Dead Arise

Dear reader, death is the strongest enemy that faces human kind. It breaks our hearts and fills us with sadness and great grief, especially when it takes those dearest to us. This is what happened to my wife and I in the summer of 1985 after our one-year-old son died in a drowning accident.

Our son Joshua was a beautiful, happy baby, our first born son. It was on his first birthday that my wife was visiting at a friend's house to celebrate the first anniversary of his life. While my wife was busy talking with her friend, she did not notice that Joshua had crawled away from her. When she realized that he was not near by, she got up to look for him. Thinking that he was exploring the house, she went in and out of each room looking and calling for him. When she could not find him, she became alarmed and ran out to the street to search for him. She called for him loudly but there was no answer. When she came back to the house she ran to the backyard. She saw something floating in the pool. She became frantic when she realized that it was Joshua. Hysterically, she grabbed him out of the pool. His small body was limp and lifeless in her arms.

The paramedics were called immediately. They tried to resuscitate him but there was no response. After forty-five minutes of trying unsuccessfully to revive him, they pulled a blanket over his head and told my wife to notify me of his death.

I was at a pastor friend's house when my wife called. I answered the phone and she sobbed, "Your son is dead, your son is dead." As she repeated these words everything in me froze. I couldn't contain my emotions and broke down. My friend tried to comfort me. We quickly left to go to them.

When we arrived at the house, I saw a large group of people in the driveway. My wife was on the ground crying loudly over our son's lifeless body. My heart was crushed to see that they had already placed him in a body blanket. Seeing the blanket draped over my son's lifeless body and hearing my wife sobbing desperately caused me more anguish than I had ever known in my life.

I got out of the car and ran to my wife. While I was trying to hold and comfort her, I thought about the times Jesus had raised the dead. Then I recalled the Scripture, **"Jesus is the same yesterday, today, and forever"** (Hebrews 13:8). At this, I was emboldened to pray over my son believing strongly that God could raise him back to life. I fell on my knees and cried out, "Oh, Jesus Christ, you are the same yesterday, today and forever. Show me your glory." Just as I ended the prayer we heard my son's cry from under the blanket. The gasping and crying increased. Everyone present heard him. The paramedics quickly pulled our son from the body blanket and began to examine him. Everyone was shocked to see that our son was breathing! As he was coughing and sputtering, trying to expel the water that was lodged in his lungs, the paramedics rushed him to the hospital.

My wife and I followed the paramedics to the hospital. It seemed like an eternity when the doctor finally came out of the emergency room. He showed us a bucket filled with water and said, "This water was inside of your son."

Many Christian people from the community and our congregation arrived at the hospital to pray with us. While the hospital personnel were still working with our son, the doctor sat down to talk with us. He cautioned us that there was a high probability that our son had sustained brain damage resulting from a lack of oxygen. He told us that our son could be left with serious disabilities such as blindness, deafness, inability to walk and neurological problems. We were even told that he may not remember us. When I heard the doctor's words I knew that God expected me to do something.

As soon as the doctor left, my wife and I urgently sought the Lord in prayer. We renewed our promise to God to follow His calling for our life. We pleaded with God, asking, even begging Him to spare our son. After what seemed like an eternity, we were finally allowed to see our son. We found him lying still in a coma. There were many intravenous lines and monitors attached to his little body. We sat next to him waiting and praying silently for God's mercy. Hours passed and although our son was breathing, he did not respond to us or the hospital personnel. It was late when the doctor came into the room and urged us to go home and get some sleep.

We went home, but we could not sleep. Fearing the possibility of memory loss and that our son may not even know us, we could not rest. So we returned to the hospital. Again we sat by Joshua's bedside and pleaded with God to complete the healing that He had begun. After awhile my wife got up. She went to Joshua's bed and gently shook him. Then, as if awakening from a deep sleep, Joshua opened his eyes, saw her, and smiled! My wife was so overcome that she picked him up off the hospital bed and began caressing him and parading him around the room. My wife was screaming with joy while little Joshua began merrily babbling and laughing! **"And He said, 'Young man, I say to you, arise.' So he who was dead sat up and began to speak. And He presented him to his mother"** (Luke 7:14-15).

The many tubes and machines that were attached to Joshua immediately sounded their alarms. The doctors and nurses rushed into the room to see what was happening. They were stunned to find little Joshua in his mother's arms, awake and alert, happily interacting with her. Joshua not only clearly remembered his mother, but he behaved as if nothing had happened to him! Our baby boy had come back to us. He had been dead, but now he was fully alive!

Soon everyone in the hospital came to see Joshua playing with his mother. The doctor examined him and told us that our son had completely recovered! Even more, he told us that our son showed no sign of neurological deficits of any kind. The doctor was so amazed that he boldly declared, "I have heard of miracles before, but this time I have seen one with my own eyes."

Joshua stayed in the hospital for another 24 hours for observation, then he was released to go home. The incident caused a big stir in the community. It was covered on all the local news stations. The doctor who had cared for our son told the TV news people that Joshua had been determined clinically dead by the paramedics and that his revival and recovery was a "modern day miracle."

We knew indeed that it was the Lord Jesus who raised our son from the dead, just as He had raised the widow's son as recorded in the gospel of Luke. We can now say with the beloved apostle John, "…**That which we have seen with our eyes, which we have looked upon, and our hands have handled, concerning the Word of life…that which we have seen and heard we declare to you**" (1 John 1:1.3). Yes, dear reader, the God who has the power to raise the dead, raised our son as a testimony that He is alive and real to all who will call upon His name.

Even the Qur'an attributes Jesus with the power to raise the dead? Surat 3:49 says, "I heal those born blind, and the lepers, **and I quicken the dead.**" Who is it that can bring life to the dead? It is only God Himself. If only God has the power to raise the dead then it follows logically that Jesus is God. Mohammad never claimed to raise the dead. Mohammad himself died and to this day we have his tomb. Abu Bakr El Sadiq, the successor to the prophet Mohammad, said, "Whoever worships Mohammad, Mohammad is died, but those who worship God, God is alive forevermore."[6] This is recorded in all the Islamic history accounts and commentaries.

The Qur'an and Hadiths also state that Jesus is still alive. It says, "O Jesus! I will take thee and raise thee to Myself (Jesus is still alive)" (Q 3:55). Yet,

Mohammad is recorded as being dead. Did you ever ask yourself why Jesus, not Mohammad, is alive forever more? And why Jesus, not Mohammad, is credited with the power to raise the dead? Jesus is the only one who is able to overcome death. The Bible tells us that Jesus Christ loosed the pains of death because it was not possible that death could hold him (Acts 2:24). Jesus states, **"I am He who lives, and was dead, and behold, I am alive forevermore"** (Revelation 1:18).

The Bible tells us that those who believe in Him will be saved. Consider these words about Jesus and decide for yourself. Just as my wife and I did when we cried out in the name of Jesus to release our son from the grip of death, so you too can ask God, in the name of Jesus, to reveal His glory to you.

Do not delay, but pray the same prayer that I prayed, **"Jesus, you are the same yesterday, today, and forever, show me your glory,"** and see what He will do for you.

*"They ask thee concerning the Spirit (of inspiration). Say: "The Spirit (cometh) by command of my Lord: of knowledge it is only a little that is communicated to you, (O men!)"*

*Qur'an 17:85*

# 20

# The Holy Spirit

My wife and I had renewed our commitment to the Lord when He brought our son back to us. We knew God was calling us to start our own Arabic church. The pastor we had been working with in Cost Mesa told us about San Diego. He said there were thousands of Muslims and Arabic people with no Arabic church. We felt in our spirit that San Diego was where we needed to be. In May of 1986, we packed up our car and headed south. While we were driving, the fifth gear in our vehicle went out on us, then the fourth gear. I knew that Satan was trying to keep us from San Diego. I knew that there was a great battle for the souls of the Muslim people. Eventually the third and second gears went out on the vehicle as well. I was undeterred. I was growing more and more confident that God had a great plan for us in San Diego. Finally, when the first gear stopped working, I turned around on the freeway and drove the rest of the way in reverse.

We started the first Arabic church in San Diego at College Avenue Baptist Church. It grew to almost 300 people. I eventually went on to help plant two more Arabic churches in the area. In 1995 I graduated from Bethel Seminary with a Master of Divinity degree and in 1996, I was asked to join the Pastoral staff at San Diego First Assembly of God Church. I would lead many seminars about Islam at Christian Heritage College and Linda Vista in San Diego. We began to develop outreaches to connect the International community together, such as our International Christmas Celebration, bringing people from all nationalities together to celebrate Jesus' birth.

In 2005, the ABN (Aramaic Broadcasting Network) director called and offered me time on the air to speak to Muslims in Canada, Mexico and the United States by satellite. I prayed and asked my congregation to pray for this opportunity. The Lord answered my prayers when one of the members surprised me and bought all the equipment we would need for the studio. We started recording our broadcast. This member and his family started recording the segments, and we sent them to the ABN.

A few years later the ABN started broadcasting in the Middle East. Our TV program, called *"The Law and the Testimony,"* was now being broadcast in the Middle East, reaching more than 30 million Muslims! I could not believe all that God was doing.

One of our goals is to show Muslims that there are many from their religion who are coming to know the Lord. We invite Muslims who have converted to Christianity to share their testimonies and their stories. We receive many responses and many questions from Muslims around the world. I also teach from the Bible, comparing the Qur'an and the Bible. I try to clearly answer all the objections the Muslims have regarding Christianity. We also invite Jewish believers to join us to show the world that through Christ alone peace can occur between the Jews and Arabs.

In 2006, God called me to start another ministry to Muslims. "Open The Gates" was developed to equip and train churches how to reach Muslims. I started with Maranatha Chapel, a large non-denominational church in San Diego, and I began a Muslim ministry in their church. I have been able to teach many classes at Maranatha Chapel and other churches around San Diego to educate Christians about Islam and how to reach out to the Muslim community, teaching them how to respond to the objections that Muslims have about Christianity. God has stirred many hearts with a deep love for the Muslim population. Muslims are coming to Christ in great numbers.

## AHMED AND KHADEGIAH

The names in this story have been changed for security purposes. One day as I was getting ready to go to the television station to record a broadcast, the phone rang. A lady from Morocco was on the line. "Hello, my name is Khadegiah. A woman named Isha told me about you. (Isha was a Muslim convert who had become a Christian.) My husband Ahmed and I would really like to meet with you today to learn more about Christ."

"I would like to meet with you and your husband but I have an appointment. Could we meet tomorrow?" I asked.

"Yes," she said ending the call. A few minutes later she called again and said, "My husband has left his work early to meet with you. He is already on his way home." Immediately I came under the conviction of the Holy Spirit. I felt God's Spirit telling me to forget about the television program and go meet with these two souls who were seeking salvation. I took down Khadegiah's address and said, "I will be at your home in twenty minutes." I called the studio and asked them to reschedule the taping.

On the way to their house, I asked God to forgive me for making the recording more important than two souls whose eternal destiny was hanging in the balance. I asked God to use me to help them come to know the truth of Christ and His salvation. I felt great joy and anticipation as I went to meet with them.

When I arrived at their home, Ahmed was on the street in front of his house waiting for me. He greeted me with the warm Islamic greeting, "Salam Alikom brother Daniel," meaning peace be upon you.

I retuned the greeting saying, "Wo Alikom al-salam wo

rahmato Allah wo barahkatoh."

He invited me into his home, beckoning me to enter first. I took off my shoes, as is the custom, and entered. His wife greeted us with Moroccan tea and traditional sweets. After introducing ourselves we began to talk about Morocco, Egypt and other cultural issues in the Middle East. I found out that Khadegiah's father was a famous Muslim leader in her hometown. I learned that Ahmed's father was the Imam of a mosque in Morocco. Khadegiah told me that when they lived in Morocco, she would wear the veil.

They asked me about my testimony and how it was that I had become a Christian. I shared with them that while I was reading The Lord's Prayer I found out that God was my heavenly Daddy. They asked me many questions about the prophet Muhammad, the teachings of the Qur'an and the teachings of Christianity.

They were typical Muslims, searching for the truth they did not find in Islam or in the Qur'an. They asked many questions, especially regarding the five objections that Muslims have about Christianity. I answered all their questions simply and clearly. I used both the Bible and the Qur'an to support my answers. I showed them evidence from the Bible and the Qur'an that Christ came to redeem mankind from condemnation.

When I finished answering all of their questions, I asked them if they were ready to accept Christ. They both said yes, and I led them in a prayer to receive Jesus as their personal Savior. Khadegiah was crying hard, knowing she had been deceived and deprived of the truth for so many years. We all felt the beautiful presence of God's peace filling our hearts after we prayed, and we rejoiced greatly.

After this, I would meet with them weekly, to disciple, teach and encourage them. Every time we met, we would make comparisons between Islam and Christianity. At one of our meetings the Lord led us into a discussion about the Holy Spirit.

In the Qur'an, there is a verse about the Virgin Mary which says, **"O my Lord! How shall I have a son when no man hath touched me?"** (Q 3:47). Muslims are taught that God breathed His Spirit into Mary and she became pregnant with Jesus. God's Spirit in the Qur'an, just as in the Bible, is considered to be the vessel of His miraculous power.

I shared with Khadegiah and Ahmed that just as it took God's power, through His Spirit, to cause the Virgin Mary to conceive, it is God's Spirit which enables believers to live faithful lives. I explained that God gives believers the Holy Spirit not only so we are enabled to live godly lives, but also so we are able to faithfully carry out His commission of sharing the gospel to the whole world.

I went on to explain that Jesus promised to send the Holy Spirit to us. We read in the book of Acts, "…**Being assembled together with them, He (Jesus) commanded them not to depart from Jerusalem, but to wait for the promise of the Father, 'which' He said, 'you have heard from Me…you shall receive power when the Holy Spirit has come upon you; and you shall be witnesses to Me in Jerusalem, and in all Judea and Samaria, and to the end of the earth'**" (Acts 1:4, 8). I also shared with them that God created the earth and all living things by the power of His Spirit (Genesis 1:2).

It is God's Spirit who worked to create the earth and cause the Virgin Mary to conceive Issa without having relations with a man. This same powerful Spirit is given to believers so they have the ability to live holy lives and also to accomplish His commission to evangelize the world. The Scriptures tell us that we can do nothing apart from His Spirit. Jesus says, **"For without Me you can do nothing"** (John 15:5). The book of Zechariah tells us that the Lord's will is not accomplished by human means but by God's Spirit. It reads, "'…**Not by might nor by power, but by My Spirit,' says the LORD**" (Zechariah 4:6).

## CHRIST'S COMMAND TO HIS DISCIPLES

Just before Jesus ascended to heaven He commanded His disciples not to leave Jerusalem but to wait for the appointment (mowad) of the Father. "**He commanded them not to depart from Jerusalem, but to wait for the Promise of the Father**" (Acts 1:4). Jesus knew that after His ascension, the disciples (al-hawariyun) would face much opposition. He knew that empires would come against them as well as even their own family members.

> "YOU SHALL RECEIVE POWER WHEN THE Holy Spirit HAS COME UPON YOU…."
>
> ACTS 1:8

He knew that Satan would continue to temp them in various ways. Indeed we know from history that the first Christians suffered many persecutions such as being thrown to the lions, stoned and even burned alive. Without the empowering of God's Spirit the disciples would not have been able to overcome the forces that were to come against them. God in His mercy promised the disciples the gift of the Holy Spirit so that they would be able to overcome all kinds of evils and hardships. Jesus knew that the disciples would not be able to carry out the great commission (the evangelization of the world) without the help of His Spirit. We read, **"But you shall receive power when the Holy Spirit has come upon you; and you shall be witnesses to Me in Jerusalem, and in Judea and Samaria, and to the ends of the earth"** (Acts 1:8). Jesus did not want them trying to carry out the great commission until they had the power of the Holy Spirit to do so.

After Jesus ascended to heaven we see that the disciples did exactly as Jesus had commanded them. We read, **"Then they (the disciples) returned to Jerusalem....They went to the upper room where they were staying...They all continued with one accord in prayer. When the day of Pentecost had fully come.... Suddenly there came a sound from heaven, as of a rushing mighty wind, and it filled the whole house where they were sitting. Then there appeared to them divided tongues, as of fire, and one sat upon each of them. And they were all filled with the Holy Spirit and began to speak with other tongues, as the Spirit gave them utterance"** (Acts1:12, 14, Acts 2:1-4).

The lives of the disciples changed dramatically after the power of the Holy Spirit came upon them at Pentecost. They proclaimed the gospel without fear. Though there were many enemies and many obstacles that came against them, they were able to share the truth throughout the Roman world. The Bible says about them, **"And they overcame him (Satan) by the blood of the Lamb and by the word of their testimony, and they did not love their lives to the death"** (Revelation 12:11).

By the same power of God's Spirit many Christians since that time have been able to take the gospel of the good news to the whole world. They did not need to use the sword or terrorism or political power to succeed. They needed God's Holy Spirit whom He graciously gives to all who know Him and ask for this precious gift.

I explained to Khadegiah and Ahmed that not all Christians have received this gift of the Holy Spirit because they have not asked for it. These Christians are weak in their faith and are unable to overcome the obstacles that come their way. They are not effective in proclaiming the gospel or overcoming sin in their own lives (Acts 19:1-7)

After any Christian receives the Holy Spirit, their lives are transformed just as these passages in the Scriptures tell us. At the end of my visit with Khadegiah and Ahmed, I asked them to pray for the outpouring of the Holy Spirit on their lives. I told them, **"For the promise is to you and to your children, and to all who are afar off, as many as the Lord our God will call"** (Acts 2:39). I told them to be ready to see a flooding of God's power on their lives and great refreshing from the Holy Spirit over them. I held their hands and we prayed together. I then left them to the grace of God and His peace.

Dear reader, God loves you and wants to change you. He knows that you are weak and that you can't live for Him by your own power. If you want to experience the outpouring of the Spirit upon your life, raise your voice to God and say, "Holy Spirit, come into my heart. Change my life by your power. Shape me as You wish. Conform me to be a vessel for Your purposes." As you pray this, God will hear you and He will move you from darkness to light, from slavery to freedom.

> "On the last day, the great day of the feast, Jesus stood and cried out saying, 'If anyone thirsts, let him come to Me and drink, he who believes in Me, as the Scripture has said, out of his heart will flow rivers of Living Water.'" (John 7:37-38)

*"He who comes from above is above all; he who is of the earth is earthly and speaks of the earth. He who comes from heaven is above all."*

*John 3:31*

# 21

# Jesus or Muhammad?

The phone rang in my office and it was my American friend Randy, who had attended my class. He asked me if I would be available to meet with a friend of his named Ali. Ali was a student form Saudi Arabia who had been receiving English lessons from Randy. Ali learned from Randy that I was a Muslim who had become a Christian. He told Randy that he had never heard of such a thing, for a Muslim to become a Christian.

We agreed to meet at one of the well-known universities in our city. When I met Ali, he immediately recognized my Egyptian accent. He told me that the Egyptians are well-liked and highly-respected by the Saudis. He added that we are appreciated for our clever humor. Egyptians are known all throughout the Middle East as being witty people. Some call Egypt the "Hollywood of the Middle East." We laughed over this and I could tell already that there was a connection between us.

After some time, he asked me how I came to be a Christian. I shared with him my testimony. I explained that I became a new person in Christ, enjoying the true light given to me so that I could walk the straight path of God.

I went on to tell him how I was deceived like all Muslims, believing that Christianity is a religion of infidelities, drunkenness, revelries, adulteries, weakness, malevolence, impurities, and all kinds of immorality and filth. I, like all Muslims, had been indoctrinated by the teaching of the Imams to loathe the Christians and the Jews as evil people who had corrupted the Scriptures. I was taught that the Bible was an immoral book encouraging lust and fornication. Islam had planted in me blindness to the truth of the Injil (gospel). I was afraid to read this "corrupt" book because of the filthiness it supposedly contained to bait its readers into committing sinful acts.

I explained to Ali how I decided to read the Christians' book for myself to see if these accusations were true. When I began to read the Bible I could not find any of the immoralities or debaucheries that the Imams said it contained. In fact, the more I read, the more I could see that it was indeed a Holy Book. I found in it only those things which are true, noble, virtuous and of good report (Philippians 4:8). I became captivated by its truthfulness, honesty, beauty and sweetness of words. The greatness of its words touched my heart deeply and I spent several hours a day reading it. Never once did I read anything corrupt or perverse. Solomon of old said of the Scriptures, "…I sat down under His shadow with great delight, and His fruit was sweet to my taste" (Song of Solomon 2:3). This too was my experience while reading the Scriptures of God.

I took the Bible and opened it up to the Book of Ephesians. I asked Ali to read for himself Ephesians 5:3-18 which says, "But fornication and all uncleanness or covetousness, let it not even be named among you, as is fitting for saints; neither filthiness, nor foolish talking, nor coarse jesting, which are not fitting, but rather giving of thanks. For this you know, that no fornicator, unclean person, nor covetous man, who is an idolater, has any inheritance in the kingdom of Christ and God. Let no one deceive you with empty words, for because of these things the wrath of God comes upon the sons of disobedience. Therefore do not be partakers with them. For you were once darkness, but now you are light in the Lord. Walk as children of light (for the fruit of the Spirit is in all goodness, righteousness, and truth), finding out what is acceptable to the Lord. And have no fellowship with the unfruitful works of darkness, but rather expose [them]. For it is shameful even to speak of those things which are done by them in secret. But all things that are exposed are made manifest by the light, for whatever makes manifest is light. Therefore He says: 'Awake, you who sleep, Arise from the dead, And Christ will give you light.' See then that you walk circumspectly, not as fools but as wise, redeeming the time, because the days are evil. Therefore do not be unwise, but understand what the will of the Lord is. And do not be drunk with wine, in which is dissipation; but be filled with the Spirit" (Ephesians 5:3-18).

> "And so we have the prophetic word confirmed, which you do well to heed as a light that shines in a dark place, until the day dawns and the morning star rises in your hearts."
>
> **2 Peter 1:19**

I emphasized to Ali the verses which mentioned adultery, fornication, uncleanness, covetousness, filthiness and coarseness. I asked him, "Did you notice that all these things are **forbidden,** according to the Bible?" I continued to explain to him that Paul, by the Holy Spirit, cautions believers to shun these things, because no one involved in them will inherit the kingdom of God (1 Corinthians 6:10). So then, how can Muslims accuse the Bible of being a corrupted book? And how can they accuse Christians of encouraging immorality when the Bible teaches holiness and purity and staying on the straight path? The Bible also cautions Christians not to drink liquor as we clearly see in the verse above where it says, **"Do not be drunk with wine… but be filled with the Spirit"** (Ephesians 5:18).

## The Bible and the Biggest Challenge

Ali became silent for a long time after I read these Scriptures. I looked him in the eye and asked him if he thought these were the words of a "corrupted" book. I challenged him to take the Bible for himself and turn to any page in it to see if there was any unseemly thing in it. I told him that he would quickly find for himself that the Bible only encourages walking in the straight path of God's love and purity and that it rejects all forms of ungodliness. I told him that I have read through the entire Bible and I have only found its words to be pure and true.

I urged him, *My dear friend, I encourage you to read the Bible for yourself. Get a copy and read on your own the truth of what I am saying. Do not accept the lies and deceptive words of your religious leaders. Be an honest seeker of the truth. Read the words of the Bible and you too will find* **"the way the truth and the life"** (John 14:6).

## JESUS OR MUHAMMAD

While I was talking with Ali, I felt led to compare and contrast the lives of Jesus and Muhammad. I began with the births of each man, continuing on to examine their earthly lives. There is a great difference between the two. I would like you to observe them here as I share with you the points I shared with Ali.

## BIRTHS

First of all, let us look at the birth of Jesus as recorded in both the Qur'an and the Bible. In the Qur'an (3:45) we are told that the Holy Spirit conceived in Mary the Word of God (Issa) who was sent into the world. The Qur'an says that the Virgin Mary was chosen by Allah above all other women to bear the seed of the chosen One. We read, **"O Mary! Allah hath chosen thee and purified thee—chosen thee above the women of all nations"** (Q 3:42). The Bible also tells us the same thing, **"...The angel Gabriel was sent by God...to a virgin... named Mary. The angel said to her, 'Rejoice, highly favored one, The Lord is with you...You have found favor with God. And behold, you will conceive in your womb and bring forth a Son, and shall call His name JESUS....Mary said to the angel, 'How can this be, since I do not know a man?'...The angel answered, 'The Holy Spirit will come upon you...'"** (Luke 1: 26-35). In fact, the Qur'an testifies that Allah made Mariam (Mary) and her son Issa to be a sign. We read, **"And (remember) her (Mariam) who guarded her chastity: We breathed into her of Our Spirit, and We made her and her son a sign for all peoples"** (Q21:91). Muhammad even gave the name "Mariam" to chapter 19 in the Qur'an, in honor of the mother of Issa.

The birth of Muhammad was very different than the birth of Jesus. Muhammad was conceived by the union of two human parents just as any human being is conceived. His parents were not noted for being righteous people as is the Virgin Mary. In fact, we know from the historical accounts that Muhammad's parents were idol worshippers.[7]

## HOLINESS

The Qur'an and the Hadith both tell us that Jesus never sinned. The Qur'an records Him as finding no fault. In the account of the angel's declaration to Mary that her son would be holy, **"I am only a messenger from thy Lord, (to announce) to thee the gift of a holy Son"** (Q19:19). All Muslim scholars agree that the word *holy* means *sinless*. Muslim scholars also agree that the Spirit of God *cannot* sin. The Bible gives us the same witness, speaking of Jesus it says, **"(He) was in all points tempted as we are, yet without sin"** (Hebrews 4:15). **"(He) committed no sin, nor was deceit found in His mouth"** (1Peter 2:22). And Jesus says of Himself, **"Which of you convicts Me of sin? And if I tell you the truth, why do you not believe Me?"** (John 8:46).

Muhammad is described as being an average human being who was not perfect but committed the same sins that are common to all human beings. Listen to what Allah tells Muhammad to say about himself, "Say, **'I am but a man like yourselves"** (Q 18:110). In another verse we find that Allah tells Muhammad to ask forgiveness for his sins, "Patiently, then, persevere…And **ask forgiveness for thy fault,** and celebrate the Praises of thy Lord in the evening and in the morning…That Allah may **forgive thee thy faults of the past and those to follow"** (Q 40:55 and Q 48:2). The Hadith of Bukhari also records the prayer of Muhammad before he died where he pleads with the Lord, "O Lord (Allahumma), forgive me and have mercy on me and grant me heaven."[8] Only sinful man needs to ask for forgiveness. Jesus is never recorded as having to ask for forgiveness because he never sinned. Since we know that no one is sinless, except God, we can only come to the conclusion that Issa (Jesus) Himself was, and is God.

## JESUS' MIRACLES

Both the Bible and the Qur'an tell us that Jesus performed many miracles during His time on earth. Jesus healed the blind, the deaf, epileptics, lepers, the lame and the demon possessed. Jesus miraculously fed more than 5,000 people on two separate occasions. He had power over nature such as the ability to walk on water, quiet the stormy seas and raise the dead. He also had complete foreknowledge of the future. All the gospel accounts attest to this. The Qur'an also records the miracles of Jesus which we see in these verses, "I (Issa) have come to you, with a sign from your Lord, in that I make for you out of clay, as it were, the figure of a bird, and **breathe into it,** and it becomes a bird ... I **heal** those born blind, and the lepers, and I **quicken** (raise) the dead... and I **declare** to you (provide for you) what ye eat, and what ye store in your houses. Surely therein is a Sign for you if ye did believe" (Q 3:49).

All Muslims scholars agree that the power to raise the dead and to know the unseen things can only belong to God. We read, "He (Allah) says, 'Who can **give life** to (dry) bones and decomposed ones (at that)? Say, 'He will give them life Who created them for the first time!'" (Q 36:78-79). "With Him (Allah) are the keys of the **unseen**, the treasures that none knoweth but He. He **knoweth** whatever there is on the earth and in the sea" (Q 6:59). **"None in the heavens or on earth, except Allah, knows what is hidden"** (Q 27:65).

The question we must ask is: If the power to create life, heal the blind, raise the dead, and know the unseen things belong to God alone, then who is this Jesus who has this very same power? Isn't it clear to you, dear reader, that Issa Al Massieh (Jesus the Messiah) must be God who came to us in the flesh?

From Jesus' conception to His ascension we see that He was continuously accompanied by the Holy Spirit, which was attested to by all the miracles He performed. **"We gave Jesus, the son of Mary Clear (Signs) and strengthened him with the holy spirit"** (Q 2:87). When we read the accounts of the life of Muhammad in the Qur'an and the Hadith, we see that there is not even one miracle or healing that is attributed to him. Muhammad's life was empty of miracles as stated in the Qur'an 29:50.

A true prophet of God will be supported by God's power to

work through him. We know, for instance, in the life of Moses that his claims to be a prophet of God were confirmed by the miracles that he did in the sight of all Egypt. This is the case with all true prophets of God. Otherwise, how can we really know that someone is a prophet from God?

As far as Muhammad is concerned, there are no miracles recorded of him. Every time he was asked to perform a miracle he was silent or gave the excuse that, **"Signs are indeed with Allah, and I am indeed (only) a clear warner (to you of this)"** (Q 29:50). He admitted that he did not possess the knowledge of the unseen. **"Say: 'I have no power over any good or harm to myself except as Allah willeth. If I had knowledge of the unseen, I should have multiplied all good, and no evil should have touched me: I am but a warner'"** (Q 7:188).

## CHRIST'S DECLARATION OF LOVE FOR US

Whoever reads the Bible will discover very quickly God's tender love for the human beings He has created. This love is especially exemplified in Christ who made a way for us to become the sons of God. The Gospel of John tells us, **"For God so loved the world that He gave His only begotten Son, that whoever believes in Him should not perish but have everlasting life"** (John 3:16). As for Muhammad and the words of the Qur'an, we are not given any indication that Allah loves us.

I asked Ali, "Does God love you?"

He answered, "Only God knows!"

Have you, my dear reader, heard this answer as well? This is because the Muslim man or woman has no assurance of God's love for him. Islam is devoid of the love of God. Muhammad never told us about God's love, but only God's anger, vengeance, and tyranny over

> **"No one has seen God at any time. The only begotten Son, who is in the bosom of the Father. He has declared Him."**
>
> **John 1:18**

us. In Islam, we are only Allah's slaves. But the Christian has the assurance of God's love. Here is an example of God's Word to His people, "The Lord hath appeared of old unto me, saying, **'Yes, I have loved you with an everlasting love; Therefore with loving kindness I have drawn you"** (Jeremiah 31:3). The Muslim cannot find such precious words in the Qur'an or in the life or sayings of Muhammad.

## WORDS AND PARABLES OF CHRIST

Jesus' words to us recorded in the Scriptures are simple, yet powerful. Many times Jesus used parables to illustrate spiritual truths to his disciples. Parables are short stories that contain important spiritual lessons. They help the untaught to understand the love and purposes of God for their lives. Examples of these parables are seen in the Sermon on the Mount (Matthew 5,6,7), the parable of the Prodigal Son ( Luke 15), and the parable of the Good Samaritan (Luke 10:30), along with may others. No one on earth can match the wisdom and purity of Christ's words.

Muhammad's words were very different than those of Jesus'. He used his word for personal benefit and to trick his enemies. He lied in order to enslave others into Islam. Muhammad was motivated by self gratification.

I asked Ali if he knew the story of Zaynab Bint Jahsh. He told me that he did. Here is brief summary, Muhammad had an adopted son named Zeid. Zeid wed a beautiful young woman named Zaynab. Muhammad went for a visit to see his adoptive son and meet his new wife. He was immediately captivated by her and desperately desired her for himself. So he went to Zeid and told him that Allah had revealed to him that Zaynab was to be his own wife, and therefore Zeid must divorce her (Q 33:36-37). Zeid obediently divorced Zaynab whereupon she became Muhammad's wife. Even Aisha (one of Muhammad's favorite wives) said with bewilderment, "I'm surprised of Allah, who allows you to do whatever you wish to do."[9]

In great contrast, Jesus said that a man who divorced his wife to marry another was committing adultery (Matthew 19:9).

This story of Zaynab Bint Jahsh is just one example of the true nature of Muhammad. Muhammad used his "revelations" for personal gain and to satisfy his earthly appetites for lust and power. If his subjects questioned him he would say, **"But those who disobey Allah and His Messenger and transgress His limits will be admitted to a Fire, to abide therein: And they shall have a humiliating punishment"** (Q 4:14).

## No Hypocrisy or Deception in Jesus

We clearly know from history and the life of Muhammad that he was full of deceit and treachery. Muhammad taught his followers to lie and even allowed them to blaspheme (deny their faith) to prosper jihad **(Taqiyya).** If a Muslim was a prisoner of war he was instructed to say and do whatever it took to trick and confuse his enemies and advance the sword of Allah. He was also given a pardon for blaspheming if under coercion. "Any (Muslim) who… utters Unbelief except under compulsion, his heart remains firm in Faith" (Q 16:106). In other words, Allah doesn't punish those who lie under duress.

In contrast, Christ lived a completely truthful and holy life. He was free of deception, lies and the twisting of words. He told his disciples, "…Let your 'Yes' be 'Yes,' and your 'No,' 'No.' For whatever is more than these is from the evil one" (Matthew 5:37). Jesus admonishes us to say what we mean and mean what we say. We are never to say something, promise something or boast of something that is not true or that we don't intend to carry out. Jesus had harsh words for those who lived hypocritical lives (saying one thing while doing another thing). He said to the corrupt religious leaders of the time, "Woe to you, scribes and Pharisees, hypocrites! For you devour widows' houses, and for a pretense make long prayers. Therefore you will receive greater condemnation" (Matthew 23:14). The God of the Bible expects us to live in true righteousness before all men, even before our enemies.

## Murder in the Name of God?

Jihad is commanded of all believers in Islam. The goal is

to convert the world, bringing all under the dictates of Sharia law. Warring until the world is put under submission to Islam is a holy decree. We see examples of this in the wars that Muhammad fought with the Jews, Christians, and the Quraysh (Muhammad's own tribe). Islamic scholars agree that Muhammad and his followers instigated and fought no less than twenty-seven wars to conquer and subdue other nations by the sword.

On the other hand, Christ's life was free from the stain of blood. He never led a rebellion, murdered or assaulted anyone. He said to his followers, **"You have heard it said, 'You shall love your neighbor and hate your enemy.' But I say to you, love your enemies, bless those who curse you, do good to those who hate you, and pray for those who spitefully use you and persecute you"** (Matther5:43-44).

I asked Ali, "Why are there two swords depicted on Saudi Arabia's national flag?" He answered that it is a symbol of the holy wars of Islam. While Muhammad ordered the killing of all who would not bow down to him as Allah's messenger, Jesus tells us to **"...have peace with one another"** (Mark 9:50). Jesus even rebuked the apostle Peter when he tried to defend Him by striking off the ear of High Priest's servant during His arrest. He said to Peter, **"Put your sword in its place, for all who take the sword will perish by the sword"** (Matthew 26:52). Then to emphasize the point, Jesus touched the servant's ear and healed him (See Luke 22:50-51)! Muhammad on the other hand encouraged his followers to kill others. We read, **"O Messenger, rouse the Believers to the fight"** (Q 8:65). How different are the words and attitudes displayed between Jesus and Muhammad!

## MUHAMMAD'S MARRIAGES

Muhammad had eleven wives and two concubines. I asked Ali, *"How, as the supposed messenger of Allah, could Muhammad take an innocent child who was still, as the Hadith tells us, playing childhood games with her friends? How is it that a holy God could approve of such a thing when it is clearly against the laws of nature and all decency?"* Ali was puzzled and did not know how to respond.

Then I asked him, *Why did Allah grant Muhammad the right to marry an infinite number of women and his followers are only allowed four wives?* We read, **"...Marry women of your choice, Two or three or four"** (Q 4:3). The Qur'an gave Muhammad the right to take, **"(all the) right hand possess** (wives, property, the spoils of war, etc)**"** (Q 33:55). In addition to all this, Allah stated that if there was a believing (Muslim) woman who desired to have sex with Muhammad, then Muhammad could have her. **"...any believing woman who dedicates her soul to the Prophet if the Prophet wishes to wed her... in order that there should be no difficulty for thee... (for) Allah is Oft-Forgiving, Most Merciful"** (Q 33:50). It seems that Allah granted to Muhammad all fleshly indulgences.

## MUHAMMAD'S DEATH

Muhammad died and his grave is with us to this day. He died in his sins. But we know according to the Scriptures that Jesus was resurrected from the dead. Jesus died as a sacrifice to take the sins of all mankind upon Himself to satisfy God's justice. Then He rose victorious! We read about Jesus that, **"(He) was delivered up because of our offenses, and was raised for our justification"** (Romans 4:25). We also read, **"... God raised (Him) up, having loosed the pains of death, because it was not possible that He should be held by it"** (Acts 2:24).

Abu Bakr Al Sadiq, the first successor to Muhammad, made an interesting statement while addressing Muslims. He said, "Who worships Muhammad? Muhammad died and those who worship will worship God alone. God is alive and does not die."[10]

I asked Ali, "Who are you going to follow, the living One or the dead one?"

He responded "Of course I will follow the living God Almighty."

I told him, "Christ rose and is forever alive. He is the Almighty God forever. Would you rather follow Muhammad, an ordinary man, born in sin from ordinary parents, whose life was void of God's love, power, morality and true righteousness; or Christ, who was born from a virgin, lived a sinless life, exemplified God's love through His love and miracles, ransomed all mankind by dying on a cross, and then was raised from the dead as the eternal Savior of the world?"

Ali said emphatically, "I will follow the Living One!"

Praise God, the veil was lifted from Ali's heart and he was able to see the light of Christ. The veil of Islam is so strong that they can't see their way to the truth. Muslims have been made prisoners by the false claims of Muhammad. I was one of those Muslims who was blinded and unable to see the way, but I thank God that He removed the veil from my eyes and freed me with the light of His gospel (Psalm 7:124)! He desires to do this for you, too, my precious Muslim brother and sister!

> "A little while longer and the world will see Me no more, but you will see Me. Because I live, you will live also."
>
> John 14:19

DEAR READER, let me ask this same question of you. Who are you going to follow? Is it the living One or the dead one? Is it the heavenly One or the earthly one? Is it the Christ or Muhammad? Search out these things for yourself and make sure that you don't entrust yourself to a false prophet.

*"For it is the God who commanded light to shine out of darkness, who has shone in our hearts to give the light of the knowledge of the glory of God in the face of Jesus Christ."*

*2 Corinthians 4:6*

# 22

# *Adam or Christ?*

When I share with my beloved Muslim friends, I like to draw their attention to the subject of Christ's miraculous birth through the Virgin Mary. I begin with these questions, **"Why is it that, of all the prophets, only Jesus was born in this unique way, that is, without the participation of a human father?"** Why is it that the prophets Muhammad, Noah, Abraham, Ishmael, and Moses were not born in this momentous way?" This is a question that must be given serious consideration in order to know the truth. By answering these questions, I pray that the curtain will be removed and the truth regarding Christ's divinity will be revealed. God is able and ready to show Himself to all who faithfully seek Him. The Scriptures tell us, **"For it is the God who commanded light to shine out of darkness, who has shone in our hearts to give the light of the knowledge of the glory in the face of Jesus Christ"** (2 Corinthians 4:6).

Muslims respond to this question by quoting the following

verse from the Qur'an, **"The similitude of Jesus before Allah is as that of Adam; He created him from dust, then said to him: 'Be.' And he was"** (Q3:59). Muslims claim, from this verse, that Jesus and Adam were created in a similar fashion and thus conclude that they are both merely men in God's eyes. They will tell the Christian that the virgin birth does not prove that Christ is God because Adam also was born without a mother or father. On the surface this seems to make sense. But let us take a closer look. We shall see in the following discussion that Adam is not equal to Christ, but Christ is far greater.

> **"You also must beware of him, for he has greatly resisted our words."**
>
> **James 3:15**

## Adam Was Dust, the Spirit of God is Christ

The Qur'an acknowledges that Adam was created from the dust of the earth (Q 3:59). This is also in the Bible, God says, **"...The Lord God formed man of the dust of the ground, and breathed into his nostrils the breath of life; and man became a living being"** (Genesis 2:7). We see here that both the Qur'an and the Bible agree that Adam was created from the dust of the earth. Christ however was not a created being. The Gospel of John tells us that Jesus is **"He who comes from heaven is above all"** (John 3:31). We also read, **"...Jesus, who was made a little lower than the angels, and...(has) partaken of flesh and blood"** (Hebrews 2:9 and 14). The Bible tells us that Christ was not created from dust like Adam, but rather is the pre-existent God who humbled Himself to come to us in the form of a human being.

Next, let us look at what the Qur'an and the Bible have to say about the uniqueness of Christ's Spirit as opposed to Adam or any of the other prophets. According to the Quran 4:171, **"...Christ Jesus the son of Mary was (no more than) an apostle of Allah...and a spirit proceeded from Him**." In the Arabic language the word "spirit" in the previous verse is **"Ruhun Minhu"**, which means **"Allah's spirit"** or **"spirit from God."** (This term is only attributed to God Himself and is equivalent in every way to Allah.) This unique title is only given to Jesus out of all of the prophets. If Allah's spirit proceeded from Jesus and not any other person or prophet of God, then doesn't it follow that Jesus is God himself in the flesh? The Bible says it like this, **"For He whom God has sent speaks the words of God, for God gives the Spirit (to Him, Jesus) by measure"** (John 3:34). It is clear from this title that there is a huge difference between Adam and Jesus. Adam is from the dust, but **Jesus is God's Spirit.**

## ADAM WAS CREATED, CHRIST IS THE CREATOR

There is also another title that has been given to Christ in the Qur'an. We read, "O Mary! Allah giveth thee glad tidings of a Word from Him: his name will be Christ Jesus, the son on Mary, held in honor in this world and the Hereafter and of (the company of) those nearest to Allah" (Q 3:45). And also, "Christ Jesus, the son of Mary… an apostle of Allah, and **His Word,** which he bestowed on Mary" (Q 4:171). In Arabic the term *word* is *Kalimatuhuu* which means *Allah's word.* Again, Muslim scholars agree that only to Jesus was this title given. We read a similar verse in the Bible where Jesus is referred to as the **"Word of God."** We read, **"…the Word was with God, and the Word was God"** (John 1:1). We also read in Revelation 19:13 that, **"…His name is called the Word of God."** So this again puts Jesus in higher status than any other of the prophets or messengers of God.

Let us take a closer look at the word **Kalimatuhuu.** According to Muslim scholars, the Word of God does not merely mean communication such as in human speech. The Word of God is also used to denote God's *creative power.* The power to create *something out of nothing*, as only God has the ability to do. In the Qur'an we read, "…He created him (Adam) from dust, then said to him, 'Be.' And he was" (Q 3:59). Allah stated the word, **"Be!"**, and Adam became a living being! We see this creative power also attributed to the **Word of God** in the Bible. We read, **"In the beginning God created the heavens and the earth. And earth was without form and void; and darkness was on the face of the deep. And the Spirit of God was hovering over the face of the deep. Then God said, 'Let there be Light:' and there was light"** (Genesis 1:1-3). You might ask me, how can God do this? He can do this because He is God Almighty and by His command He can do anything!

Muslims scholars also agree that **the Word of God is eternal**. It always existed, even before the creation of the world (At-tabaqat al-Kubr, Vol.6.325). We see this also in the Bible where it says, **"In the beginning was the Word, and the Word was with God, and the Word was God. He was in the beginning with God. All things were made through Him; and without Him nothing was made that was made"** (John 1:1-3). So then, if the Word of God (Kalimatuhuu) and Spirit of God (Ruhun Minhu) both refer to Jesus in the Qur'an doesn't it make sense that Jesus is not merely a man or even a prophet, but God Almighty Himself, come in the likeness of man? The Bible states, **"God (sent) His own Son in the likeness of ...man...."** (Romans 8:3).

## ADAM WAS A SINNER, WHILE CHRIST IS WITHOUT SIN

Both the Bible and the Qur'an record Jesus as being sinless. Both the Bible and the Qur'an record Adam and all other human beings as being infected with of sin.

We read in the Qur'an, when the angel addresses the Virgin Mary, he says, "...I am only a messenger from thy Lord, (to announce) to thee the gift of a **holy** son" (Q19:19). Islamic scholars agree that the word **holy** means **pure from sin**. We also read in the Hadith that Jesus is the only One who was never touched by sin and was able to completely resist the temptations of the devil. Narrated by Said Ibin Al-Musayyab: Abu Huraira said, "I heard Allah's Apostle saying, 'There is none born among the off-spring of Adam, but Satan touches it. A child therefore, cries loudly at the time of birth because of the touch of Satan, except Mary and her child." Then Abu Huraira recited: "And I seek refuge with You for her and for her offspring from the outcast Satan."[11]  It is because only Christ is the sinless One.

In the Bible we read that when Adam disobeyed God the entire human race inherited the problem of sin. We read, **"...Just** as through one man sin entered the world, and death through sin, and thus death spread to all men, because all sinned" (Romans 5:12). In all of history only one man is recorded as having never sinned: Jesus Christ, the Holy One of God. We read, "(Jesus Christ) was in all points tempted as we are, yet without sin" (Hebrews 4:15). Jesus Himself boldly declared to His accusers, "Which of you convicts Me of sin?" (John 8:46). No other man in the history of mankind was able to declare this about himself.

## ADAM WAS EXPELLED FROM PARADISE, CHRIST IS ALIVE FOREVER IN HEAVEN

The Qur'an tells us that both Adam and Eve were expelled from paradise. We read, "Then did Satan make them slip from the (garden), and get them out of the state (of felicity) in which they had been. We said: 'Get ye down, all (ye people), with enmity between yourselves. On earth will be your dwelling-place and your means of livelihood- for a time'" (Q 2:36). In the Bible it is recorded like this, "Then to Adam He said, 'Because you have…eaten from the tree of which I commanded you, saying You shall not eat of it: Cursed is the ground for your sake; In toil you shall eat of it all the days of your life…' Therefore the LORD God sent him out of the Garden of Eden…" (Genesis 3: 17, 23). We see from these verses that after Adam and Eve sinned by listening to the devil, they were expelled from the garden and banished from God's presence.

The Qur'an tells us that Jesus was raised to heaven. Allah says of Jesus, "O Jesus! I will take thee and raise thee to Myself… to the Day of Resurrection" (Q 3:55). In the Bible, the angels addressed the disciples telling them, "… Men of Galilee, why do you stand gazing up into heaven? This same Jesus, who was taken up from you into heaven, will so come in like manner as you saw Him go into heaven" (Acts 1:11). In another passage of Scripture, the martyr Steven declared, "Look! I see heavens opened and the Son of Man (Jesus) standing at the right hand of God!" (Acts 7:56). Both the Qur'an and the Bible are in agreement that Jesus, not Adam has gone into heaven.

The Qur'an also tells us that Jesus, not Adam, will return on the last day (Youm El Quamah) to judge the whole world (Q 43:61). The Bible declares the same thing, "…for the hour is coming in which

**all who are in the graves will hear His (Jesus) voice and come forth - those who have done good, to the resurrection of life, and those who have done evil, to the resurrection of condemnation"** (John 5: 28-29).

My dear friend, is it not clear from these passages that Allah considers Christ far superior to Adam? Adam was expelled from Allah's presence in the garden, while Jesus was elevated to His presence in the paradise of heaven for all eternity. Adam was not given the authority of judging the world on the last day. That status has been given to Jesus, the Holy One of God. It is Adam and his sons who will be facing Jesus at the judgment day. Jesus is Adam's Lord, they are by no means equal.

## ADAM DIED, BUT JESUS RAISED THOSE IN THE GRAVE

Dear reader, please read for yourself chapter eleven from John's Gospel in the Bible and you will see in fine detail the power of Jesus' word. This chapter is about a man named Lazarus who had been dead for four days. Lazarus' sisters came to Jesus crying that their brother had died. Jesus told the sisters not to worry but to take Him to the tomb where Lazarus' body lay. Upon arriving at the tomb the Bible records that, **"… (Jesus) cried out with a loud voice, 'Lazarus, come forth!' And he who had died came out bound hand and foot with graveclothes, and his face was wrapped with a cloth. Jesus said to them, 'Loose him, and let him go'"** (John 11:43-44).

Another story is recorded in the Gospel of Luke, **"And when He (Jesus) came near the gate of the city, behold, a dead man was being carried out, the only son of his mother; and she was a widow. And a large crowd from the city was with her. When the Lord saw her, He had compassion on her and said to her, 'Do not weep.' Then He came and touched the open coffin, and those who carried him stood still. And He said, 'Young man, I say to you, arise.' So he who was dead sat up and began to speak. And He presented him to his mother"** (Luke 7: 12-15).

These two stories are recording Jesus' power to raise the dead. The Qur'an tells us that, "I (Issa) have come to you, with a Sign from your Lord, in that I make for you out of clay, as it were, the figure of a bird, and breathe into it, and it becomes a bird by Allah's leave: **And I heal those born blind, and the lepers, and I quicken (raise) the dead, by Allah's leave; and I declare to you what ye eat,**

**and what ye store in your houses. Surely therein is a Sign for you if ye did believe"** (Q 3:49).

Who is able to create life, raise the dead, heal the lame, declare the future, or reveal our inmost thoughts? Only the most gracious and highest in the entire universe; only God Himself can do this! Christ is not merely human, He is God Himself revealed to us as flesh and blood, a human being! It cannot be true that Jesus is the "similitude of Adam." They are vastly different!

## JUDGEMENT COMES THROUGH ADAM, SALVATION COMES THROUGH JESUS CHRIST

None of us are immune from the infection of sin. We are completely unable to conquer the hold it has over us. The Qur'an tells us that after Adam and Eve were banished from the garden, Eve bore Cain and Abel. Cain eventually murdered his brother Abel. The curse of a sinful nature is passed through Adam and Eve to all subsequent generations. All the trouble that we see in the world today (war, destruction, hatred, lust, selfishness, covetousness, lying, thievery, disobedience) is the result of inherited sinful nature from our forefather Adam. The Bible describes it like this, **"...as through one man's (Adam) offense judgement came to all men, resulting in condemnation"** (Romans 5:18). Because of this, we have all been expelled from God's presence.

The good news is that Jesus came to set us free so that we can now be reconciled to God. Jesus entered our world in a unique way as none other had entered. Jesus was born of the Virgin Mary through the power of the Holy Spirit. He led a sinless life and then offered His life as a payment for our sins to satisfy God's anger against us. How could Jesus lead a sinless life? The only answer is that He is God in the flesh. This is a great mystery as the Scriptures declare, **"...without controversy great is the mystery of godliness: God was manifested in the flesh"** (1 Timothy 3:16).

Jesus was not a created being like Adam. Jesus is God, manifesting Himself in the likeness of man. Because Jesus came from a heavenly branch and not an earthly one, He did not inherit our sin nature. The blood running though Jesus' veins is not the earthly blood of Adam, but the heavenly blood of the King of the universe. The devil has no power over Him. Jesus is free from the nature of sin because He is God manifested in the flesh.

As the only perfect One, Jesus was able to redeem us and reconcile us back to God. We read, "...the gift (Jesus) is not like that which came through the one who sinned (Adam). For the judgment which came from one offense resulted in condemnation, but the free gift (of Jesus)... resulted in justification" (Romans 5:16). How did Jesus bring us justification? He did it by giving His perfectly sinless life as a ransom so that the debt of our sins could be paid for. We read, "...God set forth (Jesus) as a propitiation by His blood, through faith, to demonstrate His righteousness, because in His forbearance God had passed over the sins that were previously committed" (Romans 3:25). The book of Hebrews in the Bible describes the result of Christ's momentous sacrifice. "...We have been sanctified through the offering of the body of Jesus Christ once for all" (Hebrews 10:10).

My dear friend, please remember that you and I, and all human beings, are under the curse because of Adam's sin. There is unclean blood running through our veins which has deeply infected our hearts and separated us from God. But God in His great love and mercy has made a way for us to be reconciled to Him. We read, "But with the precious blood of Christ, as of a lamb without blemish and without spot. He indeed was foreordained before the foundation of the world, but was manifest in these last times for you" (1 Peter 1:19-20). He is, "...The lamb of God who takes away the sin of the world!" (John 1:29). And, "...as many as receive Him, to them He gave the right to become children of God, to those who believe in His (Jesus) name" (John 1:12).

> "...WHOEVER drinks of THE WATER THAT I shall give him will NEVER thirst. But the WATER THAT I shall give him will become in him a fountain of WATER springing up into EVERLASTING life."
>
> JOHN 4:14

Therefore, when we who are born with Adam's unclean blood come to Christ and receive forgiveness through His atonement for us we are accepted by God forever! As we surrender to Him we experience the promise of a new nature so that we are no longer in bondage to sin. We read, **"Therefore, if anyone is in Christ, he is a new creation; old things have passed away; behold, all things have become new"** (2 Corinthians 5:17).

Dear reader, please pray this prayer with me. "Lord Jesus, reveal Yourself to me. I ask you to come into my heart. Please change me and lead me from death to life. I am lost, but now I come to you because you are the Living Word. Lord of heaven and earth, creator of the universe, who has power over all things, please come into my life to be my Savior. Please forgive me of my sins and cleanse me. Thank you for sending Jesus to die for my sins so that I can live with you forever. Amen."

*"...for all have sinned and fall short of the glory of God."*

*Romans 3:23*

# 23

# The Sins of all Prophets

In the previous chapters we examined the lives of Adam, Muhammad, and Christ. We saw that only Christ was without sin as recorded in the Qur'an and Hadith, as well as in the Bible. I challenge you to show me even one shred of evidence from any of these books that Christ committed sin. I have asked many Muslim scholars this same question, and none have been able to find one verse implicating Christ of any sin or fault. Christ's uniqueness in this way surpasses all who preceded Him and all who came after Him.

I would like to provide for you a short list that shows that even the most famous prophets sinned and were in need of forgiveness from God. This will be supported by quotes from the Qur'an and the Hadith. These are just a few of the many verses which testify to the sins of the prophets.

## Evidence that Adam sinned:

"They (Adam and Eve) said, 'Our Lord! We have wronged our own souls: If thou forgive us not and bestow not upon us Thy Mercy, we shall certainly be lost'" (Q 7:23).

## Evidence that Abraham sinned:

"And who, I hope, will forgive me my faults on the day of Judgment" (Q 26:82).

## Evidence that Jonah (Younes) sinned:

"Then the big Fish did swallow him, and he had done acts worthy of blame" (Q 37:142).

## Evidence that Moses sinned:

"He prayed: 'O my Lord! I have indeed wronged my soul! Do Thou then forgive me!'" (Q 28:16).

## Evidence that Muhammad sinned:

"(The Prophet) frowned and turned away, Because there came to him the blind man (interrupting). As to the one who regards Himself as self-sufficient, To him dost thou (Muhammad) attend; Though it is no blame to thee if he grow not (in spiritual understanding). But as to him who came to thee striving earnestly, And with fear (in his heart), Of him was thou unmindful" (Q 80: 1-2, 5-10).

"That Allah may forgive thee thy faults of the past and those to follow..." (Q 48:2).

"...ask forgiveness for the fault, and for the men and women who believe: for Allah knows how ye move about and how ye dwell in your homes" (Q 47:19).

"I am asking Allah to forgive my sins more than seventy times a day."[12]

My dear friend, can you see that the above verses clearly testify that even the major prophets sinned, just as all human beings are prone to do. Muhammad was no exception to this fact. He stated himself that he asked Allah to forgive him of his sins, "more than seventy times a day" in addition to the sins he committed in the "past and for those to follow."

We read in the Qur'an and Hadith that all the prophets sinned, we cannot find any evidence whatsoever that Jesus Christ (Issa the son of Mary) ever sinned. The Hadith records that Muhammad himself quite clearly stresses this fact. We read, "At birth all the descendents of Adam have their sides pierced by the devil...**except for the son of Mary...**"[13]

The question I would like to leave with you is this: Why do the Qur'an, Hadith, and the Bible all testify that out of all the prophets only Jesus never sinned? Is it possible for a mere human being to never commit even one sin throughout a normal lifetime?

As Muslims, Christians, and Jews, we all know that the only sinless One is God. So it stands to reason that if Jesus Christ was the only human being who never sinned, then He must be more than mere human being! In fact the Bible declares that He is the Anointed One, the Holy One from God. We read about the apostle Peter asking Jesus, **"Lord, to whom shall we go? You have the words of eternal life. We believe and know that You are the Holy One of God"** (John 6:68). Even one of Muhammad's own disciples said, "I seek refuge through (Mary's progeny) from Satan the outcast" (Q 3:36).[14] Why would anyone seek refuge through another human being unless Jesus was more than a mere human being, but in fact, the Holy One of God with the power to save?

I realize that Imams have taught for many years that it is

blasphemy to say that Jesus is God. But let me assure you that **the Bible never says that a man became God. Rather it says that God became a man. This is very different!** No human being can ever presume to become God. This indeed is blasphemy! But God can do anything He likes within the confines of His holy nature including coming to us in the form of a man! And this is what He did. God humbled Himself by coming to the earth in the form of a man. Because God is sinless, so is the man Jesus Christ! **This is the reason why Jesus was able to live a sinless life, because He is God in the flesh of a human being!**

In times past before the advent of Jesus, God communicated to us through His prophets. But He desired to reach us in a more intimate way, this time through His Word (Kalimatuhuu). The Bible tells us that, **"...The Word (Kalimatuhuu) became flesh and dwelt among us"** (John 1:14). His life on earth (as recorded in the gospels) gives us a clear picture of the true nature and character of God. We read in the gospel accounts of God's power to cast out demons, heal the lame and the sick, raise people from the dead and save us from sin and hell. We see through Jesus, God's righteous and holy nature including His justice, mercy, and compassion. Most of all, we see through Jesus' life God's intense LOVE for the human beings He has created and that He desires to be our heavenly Daddy!

The Bible tells us, **"God, who at various times and in various ways spoke in time past to the fathers by the prophets, has in these last days spoken to us by His Son, whom He has appointed heir of all things, through whom also He made the worlds; who being the brightness of His glory and the express image of His person, and upholding all things by the word of His power"** (Hebrews 1:1-3). **"But when the fullness of the time had come, God sent forth His Son, born of a woman, born under the law, to redeem those who were under the law, that we might receive the adoption as sons... crying out 'Abba (Daddy) Father'"** (Galatians 4:4-6).

Dear reader, God is Love, and because of His love He came to us in the flesh of Jesus to be our Savior. I deeply desire that this truth finds its way into your heart so that you will be able to see who Issa (Jesus) is. He is not just a prophet. He is much more than that. He is God who came in the flesh. He is your heavenly "Abba, Daddy."

"And without controversy great is the mystery of godliness: God was manifested in the flesh, justified in the Spirit, seen by angels, preached among the Gentiles, believed on in the world, received up in glory."

I Timothy 3:16

*"They say: 'Allah hath begotten a son. Glory be to Him.' Nay, to Him belongs all that is in the heavens and on earth: everything renders worship to Him."*

*Qur'an 2:116*

# 24

# Is Jesus the Son of God

Muhammad lacked understanding regarding the meaning of the phrase "Son of God." This ignorance, coupled with a desire to keep his followers from straying away from his brand of religion, gave rise to a perverted interpretation of its meaning. The prophet of Islam implies in the above passage that Christians believe that God had sexual relations with a woman which resulted in the birth of the child Jesus. We see this also in this passage of the Qur'an, **"... those (also) who say, '(Allah) hath begotten a son': No knowledge have they of such a thing, nor do their fathers. It is a grievous thing that issues from their mouths (that 'God has a son') as a saying what they say is nothing but falsehood!"** (Q 18:4-5).

## "SON OF GOD?"

This is the question that we must answer before we can make a judgment as to whether or not God can have a son. What is the

Bible's intention when Christ is referred to as God's beloved Son? Does God have a son in the sense in which Muhammad understood it?

Muhammad accused Christians of believing that God had physical relations with Mary and that Jesus was the result of this union. We read, "To Him is due the primal origin of the heavens and the earth: **How can He have a son when He hath no consort?** He created all things, and He hath full knowledge of all things" (Q 6:101). Muhammad tells his followers here that Christianity is a blasphemous religion because it believes that God had sex with the Virgin Mary. And indeed, he would be right if this was the case, but this is far, far from the truth! Christians absolutely DO NOT believe that God had relations with Mary! This is NOT what the Biblical Scriptures mean by the phrase **Son of God**.

The first verse in the Gospel of Mark says, **"The beginning of the gospel of Jesus Christ, the Son of God"** (Mark 1:1). When I first began reading the Bible I wondered what the designation, Son of God meant. I asked God to help me understand this puzzling phrase.

One of the first things God showed me was that Son of God was a figure of speech and that it was not meant to be understood literally. All languages have figures of speech, or idioms, that are peculiar to their own dialects. For example, those Muslims in the Middle East are familiar with the swimmer Abouheif who swam across the Channel of the Nile. We affectionately call him the **son of the Nile**. Does this mean that Abou's father had physical relations with the Nile River and then the Nile gave birth to Abou? Of course not!

> **"And you shall know the truth, and the truth shall make you free."**
>
> **John 8:32**

So why is the word son used in this context? This is an idiom that is used to exemplify the nature, characteristic, or primary feature of its object. When we say that Abouheif is the son of the Nile we mean that he is so intimately acquainted with the Nile that it has become like a part of his nature. He trained hard, swimming in the waters of the Nile day and night, until he was able to conquer it. The

Nile became like his father because he was trained by its waters. He grew to love, respect, and affectionately cherish the Nile, as he would a father. So we give him the title "son of the Nile" because he has proven himself worthy of it.

## THE SON IS THE RADIANCE OF GOD'S GLORY

Many cultures also refer to their citizens as being sons of their particular nation. Titles such as "sons of Egypt," "sons of Persia," and "sons of the Orient" are used to designate that they are natural citizens of their individual countries or cultures. Many of these sons bear the physical features of their particular people group. The term son identifies them as being related to the people of their individual nations. But this does not mean that they were born due to a literal physical union of the country mentioned. A country is not a human being that can have sexual relations. A country is a country. We all know and understand this.

The title son is not always to be taken literally to mean the result of a physical union. The same is true with the title, Son of God which is used in the Scriptures to refer to Christ. Christ bears the characteristics of God, His Nature, His Word, His Essence. Even the Qur'an attributes to Jesus the same attributes and abilities that only God Himself has. According to the Qur'an, verse 3:49, Jesus has the ability to know the future. According to the Qur'an 15:86, 16:17, 20 and 22:73 Jesus has the power to create life from dirt just as God created Adam. And in the Qur'an 15:23 and 36:12 the Qur'an tells us in explicit language that Jesus raised the dead. The Qur'an never gives anyone else these characteristics, not even the prophet Muhammad (Q7:188, 6:50, and 11:31). Jesus is the only one in all of history who completely personifies the nature of God. The Bible describes it, **"Who being the brightness of His glory and the express image of His person, and upholding all things by the word of His power"** (Hebrews 1:3).

If the Prophet of Islam had read the Biblical Scriptures for himself, he would have known that Son of God does not mean that God married Mary or took her as his concubine and had physical sexual relations with her. Nowhere in the entire Bible is it ever stated that God had sexual relations with anyone! This is heresy! If the prophet Muhammad was really from God, surely he would have known that the Bible never makes such a claim. Unfortunately, this terrible mistake on the part of Muhammad has left Muslims all over the world misinformed about the nature of God and the truth about what Christians believe.

Please read the story of Jesus' birth from the Gospel of Matthew and the Gospel of Luke. You will discover for yourself the false accusation which Muhammad has perpetrated among his followers regarding the birth of Christ. I say with deep regret that Satan has blinded the minds of Muslims through the false teaching they have been given regarding the virgin birth.

I was a Muslim who did not understand the truth. I was deceived by the words of the Qur'an. I too used to think that Christians believed that God took Mary as his wife and had literal sexual relations with her. But now I know that Jesus is God's Son in a spiritual sense and not a physical sense. Please take the challenge to read the gospel accounts so that you will come to know the truth of the matter.

*"O Prophet! rouse the Believers to the fight."*
*Qur'an 8:65*


*"Fight against them until there is no more*
*tumult or oppression, and Allah's religion*
*(Islam) reigns supreme."*
*Qur'an 2:193*

## 25

# Is Islam a Peaceful Religion?

Today, in many parts of the world, we see Muslims carrying out suicide missions and killing others for the false hope that Muhammad offers. This is a terrible tragedy and should not be so.

I want to share with you a true story which took place during the war between Iran and Iraq in the 1990s. It was covered on the major news stations and I watched in horror as the news correspondent reported this story.

During the war between Iran and Iraq millions of Iranian soldiers under the age of twenty were sent to fight the Iraqis. They were told that they would be going on a sacred mission for Allah. The news correspondent noticed a key around one young soldier's neck. He asked the young soldier who gave him this key. The soldier responded that it was from the Grand Ayatollah Khomeini and the President of Iran. It was given to all the soldiers when they are sent to war. He told the correspondent that he was instructed to use it to open the doors of heaven as he passed from this life to the next. The correspondent flipped over the cheap metal key and saw the writing "made in Hong Kong" on its backside. The correspondent showed a close up of the writing on TV. Of course the young soldier had no idea what the English writing said. But this shows how brainwashed many are for the cause of Allah. This sad tragedy didn't stop with the war between Iran and Iraq but has come here to us in the United States, as seen in the 9/11 attacks. Very sadly, Osama Bin Laden and affiliated groups use these very same Qur'anic verses to recruit thousands of Muslim youth to accomplish their destructive and evil plans.

> "THE THIEF DOES NOT COME EXCEPT TO STEAL, AND TO KILL, AND TO DESTROY. I HAVE COME THAT THEY MAY HAVE LIFE, AND THAT THEY MAY HAVE IT MORE ABUNDANTLY."
>
> JOHN 10:10

In the Bible Jesus tells the religious leaders regarding their concept of heaven, "...You are mistaken, not knowing the Scriptures or the power of God. For in the resurrection they neither marry nor are given in marriage, but are like angels of God in heaven" (Matthew 22:29-30).

## FAISAL

The phone rang. It was my Moroccan friend, Faisal. He asked me if I could give him a ride to the airport. He was planning to visit his relatives in Morocco. By this time I had known Faisal and his family for almost a year and we had become good friends. Without hesitation, I told him I would gladly take him to the airport. The next day, I drove to his house and picked him up.

Faisal already knew, from prior experience, that I always prayed before driving. After we buckled our seat belts, I bowed my head and lifted up a silent prayer. In addition to asking for safe passage I asked that I might have opportunity to witness to Faisal about the Lord.

As we began our drive Faisal said he was anxious to see

his family. He began to share with me interesting tidbits about Moroccan culture including the current political and economic climate. Soon the conversation turned to the topic of terrorism and its entrenchment in the Middle East.

We also discussed 9/11 and its perpetrators under the dictates of Islam. Faisal did not believe me when I told him that true Islam dictates these kinds of actions. As many moderate Muslims believe, he told me that this was an isolated incident and that it was not representative of Islam. He said that only fanatic Muslim extremists believe that Islam tells them to commit such crimes.

Faisal's response to me was typical of many moderate Muslims who do not really know what the Qur'an teaches. They have never bothered to read the Qur'an for themselves to see what it says. They also ignore or whitewash Islam's history so that they won't have to look into the truth behind the actions committed in the name of Islam.

"Faisal, how was Islam spread across the Middle East, North Africa, Southern Europe and Turkey," I asked. He was silent because he knew that Islam was spread by the sword. I asked him, "Tell me, is it true or false that Islam was spread by the sword?"

"Islam was spread by the sword during its inception, but it has become a peaceful religion and no longer advocates the forcible takeover of sovereign lands," said Faisal. "Islam is now spread peacefully through methods such as education and good deeds."

"Actually, the opposite is true. Islam, at its inception began peacefully. Then, after Muhammad was driven from Mecca and fled to Medina, he gained a substantial following. He and his new followers became an army anxious to avenge their prophet. They returned to Mecca and violently took over all the tribes in the region. Thus began his rampage of slaughter in Arabia. After Muhammad's death, for more than a millennia, the slaughtering continued until much of the known world was under its domination," I explained.

The often quoted "peace" verse in the Qur'an that says, **"There shall be no compulsion in religion"** (Q2:257). It was written *before* Muhammad was forced from Mecca. This was during the early stages of Muhammad's "revelations" or "messages" as he called them. At this time he was peacefully coexisting with the surrounding tribes of the area including the Jews and the Christians. He stated, "I am but a Warner, open and clear" (Q46:9). When he tried to convert the residents of Mecca by declaring that he was a prophet sent from God he became a laughing stock and a nuisance. Deemed a troublemaker, they chased him out and he fled to Medina. After finding a more receptive audience in Medina he built his power base. Still nursing a grudge against the tribes of Mecca for refusing to believe that he was Allah's prophet, he returned a few years later with 10,000 warriors. They laid siege to the city and in a successful campaign he installed himself as the supreme leader. This happened in January of 630AD. Islamic takeover of peoples and lands through means of the sword continued right up through the Ottoman Empire (1299-1922).

I also detailed for Faisal the succession of leadership in Islam. Muhammad died in 632 AD. Abu Baker, his father-in-law by his wife Aisha, became the second successor to Islam. He died of natural causes after two years whereupon Omar Ben Khatab became the third successor. Under his leadership, from 634-644, Islam conquered Iraq, Syria, Egypt and Jerusalem. During this time the famous Mosque called the Dome of the Rock was built. It was built on the same piece of land that housed Solomon's Temple. Omar Ben Khatab was assassinated in 644 and Othman Ben Afan became the fourth successor. After 12 years he too was assassinated. Next came Ali Aben Taleb. It was at this time (661 AD) that Islam split into two factions; Sunni and Shia. Damascus became the capital of the Islamic nation. After this, Islam invaded parts of Russia, China and much of North Africa. In 750 AD the Islamic Capital moved again, this time to Baghdad. From there Muslims went out to forcibly convert Iran, India, Spain, and France.

I asked Faisal, "Why is it that all, except one, of the first five successors to Muhammad were assassinated?" He could not answer me. "It is because Islam is built on the sword. We see this violent mentality not only in the take over of nations but also in the succession of leadership."

Faisal did not like the idea that Islam fought its way into

countries and lands. He told me, "After the first incident at Mecca, Muslims called others to peacefully submit to Islam. It was only if they refused to submit that war became necessary."

I couldn't believe what I heard him say! He was telling me that Islam was peaceful, if you submitted to it. "This makes no sense! How could something be peaceful if it is forced upon you?" I said. "Imagine that someone came to invade my house. This person knocked on my door and said, 'Daniel, I want to have your house. All I want is for you to leave peacefully. If you resist I will torture and kill you and sell your family into slavery.' Is this acceptable, my friend, for someone to simply come into my house and force it from me? Is it right that someone should take my land, the land I tended all my life, that I earned and love?" I continued, "What kind of peace is this? This man wants to steal what belongs to me. His intention is to kill me if I don't surrender my property to him. He is a thief. This is extortion, my friend, not peace!"

Faisal thought carefully about the example I gave him. Then he conceded and said, "Yes, I understand what you are saying."

Now, dear reader let me quote for you here just a few of the thirty plus Qur'anic verses that encourage terror and killing in the name of Islam:

"….**fight** and slay the Pagans wherever ye find them, and seize them, beleaguer them, and lie in wait for them in every stratagem" (Q 9:5).

"O Prophet! **Strive hard against** the unbelievers and the Hypocrites, and be firm against them. Their abode is Hell, - an evil refuge indeed" (Q9:73).

"**Fight** those who believe not in Allah nor the Last Day, nor held that forbidden which hath been forbidden by Allah and His Messenger, nor acknowledge the religion of Truth, **(even if they are)** of **the People of the Book,** until they pay the **Jizya** with willing **submission,** and feel themselves subdued" (Q 9:29).

"Against them make ready your strength to the utmost of your power, including steeds of war, to strike **terror** into (the hearts of) the enemies, of Allah" (Q 8:60).

"I will instill **terror** into the hearts of the Unbelievers: **smite ye above their necks and smite all their finger-tips off them**" (Q 8:12).

"O ye who believe! **Fight** the unbelievers who gird you about, and let them find firmness in you" (Q 9:123).

"Therefore, when ye meet the Unbelievers (in fight), **smite at their necks**; At length, when ye have thoroughly **subdued** them, bind a bond firmly" (Q 47:4).

"...**Fight** them until there is no more Tumult or oppression" (Q 2:193).

"It is not ye who slew them; it was Allah" (Q 8:17).

Is it not obvious that Allah commands Muhammad and his followers to kill the infidels including the people of the Book (Jews and Christians)? It says anyone who does not believe in Islam must be subjugated or killed (Q 9:29). Moderate and uninformed Muslims try to justify these verses by saying that these Jihad verses were only to be followed during Islam's inception. But history and the Qur'an all testify that this is not the case. The Qur'an clearly states that Jihad (war in the name of Islam) is to take place, "till the religion be for Allah" (Q 2:193), that is, until all the world is under the control of Islam. The Qur'an does not declare a particular date that Islam is to cease fighting for world control. It is only to end when, "the religion be for Allah." In other words, forced conversion is to continue until all are submitted to the will of Allah in Islam.

Regarding the earlier revelations of Muhammad, conservative Muslim theologians and clerics are in agreement that Muhammad's latter revelations *abrogate the earlier ones.* That is, the "peace" verses of Muhammad's earlier revelations *are replaced* by Muhammad's later (Jihad) revelations.

Here are several verses that state the principle of abrogation in Islamic theology:

"None of Our revelations do We abrogate or cause to be forgotten, but We substitute something better or similar: Knowest thou not that Allah Hath power over all things?" (Q 2:106).

"When we substitute one revelation for another, - and Allah knows best what he reveals (in stages), - they say: 'Thou art but a forger": but most of them understand not" (Q 16:101).

"Allah doth blot out or confirm what He pleaseth: with Him is the Mother of the Book" (Q 13:39).

"If it were Our Will, We could take away that which We have sent thee by inspiration: then wouldst thou find none to plead thy affair in that matter as against Us" (Q 17:86).

So we see here, based on the principle of abrogation, that, "there shall be no compulsion in religion" is superseded by, "fight and slay the pagans... seize them... lie in wait for them in every stratagem... instill terror into the hearts of the unbeliever...O Prophet, rouse the believers to the fight."

Let me ask another question. Why is it that Christianity has become the dominant religion in the world without force? Why was Jesus able to gain so many converts without lifting the sword? How is it that even in spite of the torture and martyrdom of Christians down through the ages, it prevails?

You may be asking, "But what about the Crusades? Weren't they done in the name of Christ?" The Crusades were carried out highly inappropriately. The leaders of this era (1095-1291) who instigated the Crusades were not really true Christians. They *used* the name of Christ to propagate their own lust for power. *But what they did is clearly against the teachings of Christ!* If you take the time to read the New Testament for yourself, you will see that what they did is contrary to everything Jesus stands for.

Christ is the true Prince of Peace who came to sacrifice Himself for mankind. He did not lead a rebellion to gain power and lands. He never killed anyone. He never hurt anyone. We read, **"Jesus of Nazareth...went about doing good and healing all who were oppressed by the devil, for God was with Him"** (Acts 10:38). He did this to, **"...gather together in one the children of God who were scattered abroad"** (John 11:52). Jesus called for peace, love and forgiveness. Jesus taught in the Sermon on the Mount, **"You have heard that it was said, 'You shall love neighbor and hate your enemy.' But I say to you, love your enemies, bless those who curse you, do good to those who hate you, and pray for those who spitefully use you and persecute you"** (Matthew 5:43-44). He also taught, **"You have heard that it was said to those of old, 'You shall not murder, and whoever murders will be in danger of the judgment.' But I say to you that whoever is angry with his brother without a cause** shall be in danger of the judgment. And whoever says to his brother, 'Raca!' shall be in danger of the council. But whoever says, 'You fool!' shall be in danger of hell fire" (Matthew 5:21-22).

We also read that God loves His creation and wants us to have eternal life with Him. We read, "For God so loved the world that He gave His only begotten Son, that whoever believes in Him should not perish (in hell), but have everlasting life (in heaven)" (John 3:16). "The Lord is not slack concerning His promise…but is longsuffering toward us, not willing that any should perish but that all should come to repentance" (2 Peter 3:9). What heavenly words these are, free from the language of murder, war, abuse and hate. Love is the language of the Lord of Heaven. Murder and hatred are the language of the devil.

After the events of September 11, 2001, many Muslims around the world were anxious to disassociate themselves from the connection between terrorism and Islam. We began to hear slogans like, "Islam is a religion of peace." Those who carried out the attacks on 9/11 were branded as extremists and outlaws of true Islam. Unfortunately, many Muslims (and Western world leaders) believe these lies because they are not familiar with the Qur'an. They do not realize that what these terrorists did was due to the demonic influence of the Qur'an's teachings.

One of the key pillars of Islam is "Jihad," which means to kill for the sake of Allah. War, sabotage, murder, enslavement, terrorism and rape are all justified by the Qur'an as means to unify the world under the banner of Islam. The 9/11 hijackers all fell under the spell of the Qur'an's influence taught by the Imams who propagate its teachings.

Clearly the book of the Qur'an is not from God. At one time I believed in the teachings of the Qur'an. I never doubted that they came from God. But when God opened my eyes and the light of Christ dawned upon me I was able to judge that something was amiss from it. I saw that it was not from a God who truly loved me and cared for me but rather from an earthly diabolism. Satan used the prophet of Islam to kill in the name of religion. He inspires the followers of Islam not only to kill non-Muslims but to kill Muslims of a different sect as well. See what is happening this very day in countries such as Iraq, Lebanon and Afghanistan? This is a jihad of Muslim against Muslim!

Concerning the devil, the Bible says, **"The thief does not come except to steal, and to kill, and to destroy"** and **"He was a murderer from the beginning, and does not stand in the truth, because there is no truth in him. When he speaks a lie, he speaks from his own resources, for he is a liar and the father of it"** (John 10:10 and John 8:44). Jesus never instructs His followers to kill, to steal or to destroy. How different are the words of Muhammad.

Sadly, violence and destruction is the outcome of the Islamic religion. I do not say this to anger you, but to advise you because I love you and do not want you to suffer loss. Read the Bible for yourselves to verify the truth of what I am telling you. Come to the true God and ask Him to open your eyes and heart, so that you too will come to know true peace that only He can give you.

*"For the wages of sin is death, but the gift of God
is eternal life in Christ Jesus our Lord."*

*Romans 6:23*

# 26

# Why Mohammad Came

The phone rang and when I picked up the receiver it was my Iraqi friend, Ali, on the line. Ali invited my family to join his family for a picnic at a park in our town. I thanked him for his invitation and agreed to meet the following Sunday at noon by the water.

I brought with me my wife and her lovely mother. We met Ali, his wife and their children. It was a beautiful, peaceful day. There was nothing to interrupt us but the quiet lapping of water and the distant sound of vessels passing. We sat on the ground while my friend skillfully grilled a large batch of fresh fish. The women prepared the rest of the food and we sat down for a wonderful meal.

We were chatting about various things when my mother-in-law began sharing about the times when Jesus had appeared to her. She shared about a time when a pot of boiling water fell on her daughter. Her daughter was burned severely on her face and left hand. She took her to the hospital for treatment. While at the hospital the Lord appeared to her. He told her that her daughter would be healed that very day from the burns she sustained and that there would be no scarring. She said the Lord told her that this would happen after she shared the good news about Jesus to the people around her in the hospital. So she told everyone in the hospital about Christ and His work in her life. She told many patients and their families, as well as many of the hospital personnel. Soon after sharing about Jesus, the doctors came and reported to her that her daughter was completely healed. In fact, she showed no signs of ever having been burned!

Ali and his wife were touched by this story. Then Ali asked me, "How many books are written about Jesus in Christianity?"

I told him, "There are four gospels which were written by Jesus' closest followers called disciples. The disciples accompanied Jesus throughout his earthly ministry and were intimately acquainted with him. They recorded many things in the life of Jesus which include His miracles and healings as well as His death, resurrection and ascension into Heaven. Each disciple wrote the same story yet each wrote with their own particular emphasis. For example, Matthew wrote much about Jesus as the King of Kings. Mark wrote about Jesus as the obedient Servant of God. John wrote to us much about God's great love. Each disciple wrote a diary of Jesus' life. And even though each diary has its own personality and perspective, the stories are all in agreement with each other. There are no contradictions."

I went on to tell him, "The four gospels complement each other and whoever reads them will see a complete picture of the life of Jesus. The reader will learn who Jesus Christ is, why He came into the world and how His work on the cross provided salvation for all mankind. God came to us incarnated in the form of a man. God has the ability to do anything and be everywhere at the same time. He chose to reveal Himself to us 2000 years ago in a way that we could understand, in the person of Jesus. Jesus led a perfectly sinless life, took upon himself the penalty for our sins, thereby satisfying God's wrath against us, and reconciling us to God. God's all encompassing love for us compelled Him to do this magnificent thing!

## MOMENTOUS SACRIFICE

My mother-in-law asked Ali, "Is it true that the Qur'an tells the story of Abraham having a dream where Allah tells him to sacrifice his son? And that just as Abraham was about to slay his son, Allah called out to him saying, "'O Abraham! Thou hast already fulfilled the vision!'...and We ransomed him (Abraham's son) with a **momentous sacrifice**" (Q 37:104-105, 107)?

Ali answered, "Yes, this is what the Qur'an says."

Then my mother-in-law asked him, "What was this momentous sacrifice?"

Ali responded, "The momentous sacrifice refers to the ram that Allah provided for Abraham to slay instead of his son."

Then my mother-in law-said to Ali, "Yes, this is true, but why would Allah call a lowly animal a momentous sacrifice? Could a mere animal be a momentous sacrifice? Of course not. An animal is not greater than a man, and a man is not greater than God. The only one who is truly momentous is God. So how could God be a sacrifice? The ram God provided for Abraham to sacrifice was a precursor to Jesus' sacrificial death on the cross. Ali, the Bible says of Jesus, **"Behold! The Lamb of God who takes away the sin of the world"** (John 1:29). Jesus' death on the cross was the momentous sacrifice, the momentous ransom for our souls."

From this point I began to tell Ali that all human beings are in need of a great sacrifice. We all have committed sins and have transgressed God's perfect law. The Bible says it this way, **"Every one of them has turned aside; they have together become corrupt; there is none who does good, no, not one"** (Psalm 53:3). Because of this we all deserve punishment and doomsday. We have all insulted God's holiness through the sins we have committed. God's righteousness demands a payment for the sins we have committed against Him. And that punishment is eternal death or separation from God.

The Qur'an tells the tragic story of the fall of Adam and Eve from the garden (Q 2:36). This story is also a key text of the Bible. (Genesis 3) After Adam and Eve sinned, God had to expel them from the Garden of Eden because He cannot look upon sin. Separation from God was their consequence. Because we have all inherited sin through Adam and Eve we are all under the same condemnation.

So then, how can we escape the punishment of eternal death (which is separation from God)? The Bible tells us, "… **while we were still sinners, Christ died for us**" (Romans 5:8). These are the most beautiful words. Because God loves us and does not want us to spend eternity in hell, separated from Him, He sent His Son **Jesus as the momentous sacrifice** to ransom us! God sent Christ to carry our sins to the cross and open the door of paradise to all those who believe in His Name.

I gave Ali an example of a substitute paying a debt. I said to Ali, "Let's say you owed a creditor a hundred dollars that you could not pay. You were just about to be thrown in jail, when someone came forward and said, 'I will pay the debt for you.' Once the debt was paid, the creditor could no longer send you to jail. This is what Christ did by taking the sins of all mankind to the cross. We are free from the punishment of eternal death if we simply receive this great gift!"

The Bible tells us, "**For the wages of sin is death, but the gift of God is eternal life in Christ Jesus**" (Romans 6:23). We are also told, "**There is therefore now no condemnation to those who are in Christ Jesus our Lord**" (Romans 8:1). God sent Jesus to die in our place because He loves us! We read, "**For God so loved the world that He gave His only begotten Son, that whoever believes in Him should not perish but have everlasting life**" (John 3:16).

The realization of Christ's momentous sacrifice flashed in Ali's mind and suddenly he asked an important question, "**If what you are saying is true, for what purpose did Muhammad come to us? If Christ already opened paradise for us, why do we need the prophet Muhammad?**" Ali realized at that very moment that Muhammad did not give us anything!

I told Ali, "You have rightly judged the matter. I encouraged you to read the Bible for yourself." I gave him a copy of the New Testament which he received with much appreciation.

My dear reader, Ali was able to distinguish between Muhammad and Christ with the simple question, "Why did Muhammad come?" I encourage you to ask the same question — with all sincerity. Was there anything unique that Muhammad brought to benefit humanity? Why would God need to send another prophet if Christ is already the Savior of the world? Salvation has been completed. Scripture tells us that Christ **"...with His own blood... entered the Most Holy Place once for all, having obtained eternal redemption"** (Hebrews 9:12). Christ Himself said, **"...It is finished"** (John 19:30).

God loves you and does not want you to die in your sins. He prepared salvation for you with the momentous sacrifice of His Son. Yes, Christ's blood is what can save you from God's wrath. The Bible tells us, **"Nor is there salvation in any other, for there is no other name under heaven given among men by which we must be saved"** (Acts 4:12). Muhammad did not bring anything to help the condition of mankind. All the good works Muhammad did (fasting, prayer, charity, and observing dietary restrictions) do nothing to correct the real problem of the human condition. The law was already established by the prophet Moses a thousand years before Muhammad. The Mosaic Law also could not make us pure before God. The purpose of the law was to show us that no matter how hard we try, we cannot measure up to God's standards. Scripture tells us that God gave the law to help us realize that we need a Redeemer. We read, **"But before faith came, we were kept under guard by the law, kept for the faith which would afterward be revealed. Therefore the law was our tutor to bring us to Christ, that we might be justified by faith"** (Galatians 3: 23-24).

Perhaps you think that your good works will outweigh your sins and that by this you will obtain salvation. But the Bible tells us that in God's eyes, **"...all our righteousnesses are like filthy rags; we all fade as a leaf, and our iniquities, like the wind, have taken us away"** (Isaiah 64:6). Let me give you a simple example. Let us say that you committed a crime. You stand in front of the judge while the evidence against you is presented, proving that you are guilty of the crime. Then, it is your turn to defend yourself. You begin telling the judge about all your good works before you violated the law. Do you think the judge will be impressed? No! Because the fact is, you still committed the crime! It is the same with us before God. No matter how many good works we have done in our lifetime we have all fallen short of God's perfect standards. We can never justify ourselves before God on our own merits.

So, what then is the solution? What is the way of escape? The Bible tells us that the only way of escape is through the precious blood of Jesus that was shed for every human being. Jesus said, **"I am the way, the truth, and the life. No one comes to the Father except through Me"** (John 14:6). Christ already received the punishment for our sins. He alone appeases God's justice. And He alone will save you through faith in Him.

*"For inquire, please, of the former age, And consider the things discovered by their fathers."*

*Job 8:8*

# 27

# *Is the Qur'an the Word of God?*

The Qur'an declares it is from God proven by the fact that its words and thoughts contain no discrepancies, impurities or contradictions. It stands to reason that if a book is from God, who is perfect, then its words and thoughts will also be pure and perfect.

I took the opportunity to put the Qur'an to the test and did my own exhaustive research. I would like to show you what I discovered. I encourage you to check the accuracy of my research for yourself. After all, it is the Qur'an that is challenging you to the task of finding out if Muhammad's revelations are from God or not.

Let us take a few subjects and look at the verses in the Qur'an that address them.

We will do this by asking a question of the Qur'an and then looking to the answers that it provides. Please see if you notice any discrepancies or attributes that would be contrary to the character of a pure, perfect, and holy God. For your convenience I have placed in bold the keywords pertaining to the subject being looked at. I have italicized (also in bold) any words that seem to contradict previous keywords. These contradictions may appear within the same verse. After examining the verses, I will offer a summary and conclusion. Please see if you agree with my conclusions.

## QUESTION ONE: WHAT IS THE SPAN OF A DAY FROM ALLAH'S PERSPECTIVE?

"He rules (all) the affairs from the heaven to the earth; in the end will (all affairs) go up to Him, on **a Day, the space whereof will be (as) a thousand years** of your reckoning" (Q32:5).

"The angels and the Spirit ascend unto Him in **a Day the measure whereof is (as) fifty thousand years**" (Q70: 4).

**Summary:** In the first verse we read that a day is 1,000 years. In the second verse we read that a day is 50,000 years.

**Conclusion:** There is a discrepancy as to the span of Allah's day.

## QUESTION TWO: CAN ALLAH HAVE A MEDIATOR?

"Say: **'To Allah belongeth exclusively (the right to grant) intercession.** To Him belongs the dominion of the heavens and the earth: In the End, it is to Him that ye shall be brought back" (Q 39:44).

"It is Allah Who has created the heavens and the earth, and all between them, in six Days, and is firmly established on the Throne (of Authority): **ye have none, besides Him, to protect or intercede (for you):** will ye not then receive admonition?"(Q32:4).

"Verily your Lord is Allah, who created the heavens and the earth in six days, and is firmly established on the throne (of authority), regulating and governing all things. **No intercessor (can plead with Him) except after His leave (hath been obtained).** This is Allah your Lord; Him therefore serve ye: will ye not receive admonition?" (Q 10:3).

**Summary:** The first two verses emphatically state that only Allah can be a mediator. The third verse tells us that Allah allows a mediator "to save after His permission."

**Conclusion:** The Qur'an gives contradictory messages regarding whether or not there is another mediator besides Allah.

## QUESTION THREE: HOW MANY MUSLIMS WILL INHERIT HEAVEN?

"These will be those Nearest to Allah. In Gardens of Bliss: A number of people from those of old (People of the Book), and **a few from those of later times**" (Q 56:11-14).

"For the Companions on the Right Hand. A (goodly) **number from those of later time**" (Q56: 38-40).

**Summary:** The first verse tells us that only "a few" Muslims will be present in heaven. The second verse tells us that "a multitude" of Muslims will be in heaven.

**Conclusion:** The Qur'an presents contradictory messages regarding whether there will be many Muslims in heaven or only a few.

# QUESTION FOUR: WHO INHERITS HEAVEN, MUSLIMS ALONG WITH THE PEOPLE OF THE BOOK, OR MUSLIMS ONLY?

**"Those who believe (in the Qur'an), and those who follow the Jewish (scriptures), and the Christians and the Sabians,-** any who believe in Allah and the Last Day, and work righteousness, **shall have their reward with their Lord;** on them shall be no fear, nor shall they grieve" (Q2:62).

**"If anyone desires a religion other than Islam (submission to Allah), never will it be accepted of him;** and in the Hereafter He will be in the ranks of those who have lost (All spiritual good)" (Q3:85).

**Summary:** The first verse tells us that all who believe in God including the Jews, Christians, and Sabians will be in heaven. The second verse tells us that only those who believe in the religion of Islam will be admitted into heaven.

**Conclusion:** There is a discrepancy regarding exactly who will be present in heaven.

# QUESTION FIVE: IS MUHAMMAD COMMANDED TO OVERLOOK THE FAULTS OF OTHERS OR TO FIGHT HARD AGAINST THEM?

"We created not the heavens, the earth, and all between them, but for just ends. And the Hour is surely coming (when this will be manifest). **So overlook (any human faults) with gracious forgiveness**"(Q15:85).

**"O Prophet! strive hard against the unbelievers and the Hypocrites, and be firm against them.** Their abode is Hell, - an evil refuge indeed" (Q9:73).

**Summary:** In the first verse we see Allah telling Muhammad to be merciful and overlook the faults of others (without a qualifier we can assume that this includes unbelievers). In the second verse we see Allah telling Muhammad exactly the opposite.

**Conclusion:** The Qur'an gives contradictory messages regarding whether to forgive and be lenient to unbelievers or to punish and subjugate them.

## QUESTION SIX: DOES ALLAH FORBID ADULTERY OR DOES HE ALLOW IT?

"When they do aught that is shameful: 'We found our fathers doing so'; and '(Allah) commanded us thus': Say: **'Nay, Allah never commands what is shameful;** do ye say of Allah what ye know not?'" (Q7:28).

**"Also (prohibited are) women married, except those whom your right hands possess: Thus hath Allah ordained (Prohibitions) against you.** Except for these, all others are lawful, provided ye seek (them in marriage) with gifts from your property, - desiring chastity, not lust, seeing that ye derive benefits from them, give them their dowers (at least) as prescribed; but if after a dower is prescribed, agree Mutually (to vary it) here is no blame on you, and Allah is All-knowing, All-wise" (Q 4:24).

**"O Prophet! We have made lawful to thee thy wives to whom thou hast paid their dowers; and those whom thy right hand possesses out of the prisoners of war whom Allah has assigned to thee;** and daughters of thy paternal uncles and aunts, and daughters of thy maternal uncles and aunts, who migrated (from Mecca) with thee; and any believing woman who dedicates her soul to the Prophet if the Prophet wishes to wed her;- this only for thee, and not for the Believers (at large); We know what We **have appointed for them** as to **their wives and the captives whom their right hands possess;**- in order that there should be no difficulty for thee. And Allah is Oft-Forgiving, Most Merciful" (Q 33:50).

"Thou mayest defer (the turn of) any of them that thou pleasest, and **thou mayest receive any thou pleasest, and there is no blame on thee if thou invite one whose (turn) thou hadst set aside.** This were nigher to the cooling of their eyes, the prevention of their grief, and their satisfaction - that of all of them - with that which thou hast to give them: and Allah knows (all) that is in your hearts: and Allah is All- Knowing, Most Forbearing" (Q 33:51).

**Summary:** On the one hand believers are told that they are prohibited from taking married women as wives. Then we see a qualifier that gives permission for the believer to take any married women he likes who has been captured in war ("whatever thy right hand possesses").

**Conclusion:** Allah allows adultery.

## QUESTION SEVEN: ALLAH SWEARS BY WHAT CITY?

"I (swear by) **this City of security (Mecca)**" (Q 95: 3)

"I do not call to witness **this City**" (Q 90: 1).

**Summary and Conclusion:** In one verse Allah is swearing by the city Mecca and in another verse he does not swear by the city, therefore, contradicting himself, and is indecisive.

## QUESTION EIGHT: DOES ALLAH FORBID DECEPTION OR DOES HE ALLOW IT?

"**To the Hypocrites give the glad tidings that there is for them (but) a grievous penalty**" (Q4:138).

"Any one who, after accepting faith in Allah, utters Unbelief, except under compulsion, his heart remaining firm in Faith - but such as open their breast to Unbelief, on them is Wrath from Allah, and theirs will be a dreadful Penalty" (Q16:106).

**Summary:** It is permissible in Islam to make a false confession under certain circumstances.

**Conclusion:** Allah allows deception.

## QUESTION NINE: ARE MUSLIMS TAUGHT TO PERSUADE NON-BELIEVERS WITH WORDS OR WITH THE SWORD?

**"Let there be no compulsion in religion**: Truth stands out clear from Error: whoever rejects evil and believes in Allah hath grasped the most trustworthy hand-hold, that never breaks. And Allah heareth and knoweth all things" (Q 2: 256).

**"Invite (all) to the Way of thy Lord with wisdom and beautiful preaching;** and argue with them **in ways that are best and most gracious**: for thy Lord knoweth best, who have strayed from His Path, and who receive guidance" (Q16:125).

"And **fight them on until** there is no more Tumult or oppression, and **there prevail justice and faith in Allah,** but if they cease, Let there be no hostility except to those who practice oppression" (Q 2:193).

**"Fight those who believe not in Allah**, nor the Last Day, nor hold that forbidden which hath been forbidden by Allah and **His Messenger**, nor acknowledge the religion of Truth, (even if they are) of the People of the Book, until they pay the Jizya with willing submission, and feel themselves subdued" (Q9:29).

**Summary:** In the first two verses we see that Islam is not to be forced upon unbelievers. In the second two verses we see that Islam is to "fight those who do not believe in Allah."

**Conclusion:** The Qur'an gives contradictory messages regarding methods (peaceful verses violent) of converting unbelievers. The majority of verses favor violence.

## QUESTION TEN: DID PHARAOH DIE OR DID HE ESCAPE DEATH AFTER PROFESSING FAITH IN ISLAM?

"We took the Children of Israel across the sea: Pharaoh and his hosts followed them in insolence and spite. At length, when overwhelmed with the flood, he said: 'I believe that there is no god except Him Whom the Children of Israel believe in: I am of those who submit (to Allah in Islam).' (It was said to him): 'Ah now! - But a little while before, wast thou in rebellion!- and thou didst mischief (and violence)! **This day shall We save thee in the body, that thou mayest be a sign to those who come after thee!** but verily, many among mankind are heedless of Our Signs!'" (Q10: 90-92).

"Moses said, "Thou knowest well that these things have been sent down by none but the Lord of the heavens and the earth as eye-opening evidence: and I consider thee indeed, O Pharaoh, to be one doomed to destruction!" So he resolved to remove them from the face of the earth: but **We (Allah) did drown him and all who were with him**" (Q17:102-103).

**Summary:** In the first verse we see that Allah saved Pharaoh because he submitted to "Allah in Islam." In the second verse we see that Allah caused Pharaoh to drown in the sea.

**Conclusion:** The Qur'an gives contradictory accounts regarding Pharaoh's outcome.

# QUESTION ELEVEN: IS ALLAH'S WORD PURE AND FIXED OR IS IT IMPURE AND SUBJECT TO CHANGE?

"And when Our Clear Signs are rehearsed unto them, those who rest not their hope on their meeting with Us, Say (O Muhammad): '**Bring us a reading other than this, or change this,"** Say: 'It is not for me, of my own accord. I follow naught but what is revealed unto me:** if I were to disobey my Lord, I should myself fear the penalty of a Great Day (to come)" (Q10:15).

"And **recite (and teach) that which has been revealed to thee of the Book of thy Lord: none who can change His Words,** and none wilt thou find as a refuge other than Him" (Q18:27).

"We have, without doubt, **sent down the Message; and We will assuredly guard it (from corruption)**" (Q 15:9).

"**When we substitute one revelation for another,** - and Allah knows best what He reveals (in stages), - they say, 'Thou art but a forger': but most of them understand not" (Q16:101).

"**None of our revelations (even a single verse) do We abrogate or**

**cause be forgotten, but We substitute something better or similar:** Knowest thou art not that Allah Hath power over all things" (Q 2:106).

"**Allah doth blot out or confirm** what He pleaseth: with Him is **Mother of the Book**" (Q 13:39).

"O Prophet! We have made lawful to thee thy wives to whom thou hast paid their dowers; and those whom thy right hand possesses out of the prisoners of war whom Allah has assigned to thee; and daughters of thy paternal uncles and aunts, and daughters of thy maternal uncles and aunts, who migrated (from Mecca) with thee; and any believing woman who dedicates her soul to the Prophet if the Prophet wishes to wed her;-**this only for thee, and not for the Believers (at large)**" (Q 33:50).

**Summary:** In the first three verses we are told that Allah's word cannot be changed. In the next three verses we see that Allah changes his word for "something better." In the last verse we see that Allah's word changes specifically to meet the prophet Muhammad's lust.

**Conclusion:** Allah's word is not pure. It changes as it caters to Muhammad's whims.

## QUESTION TWELVE: WHAT IS ISLAM'S HEAVEN LIKE?

"They (those in heaven) will recline on Carpets, whose inner linings will be of rich brocade: the Fruit of the Gardens will be near (and easy of reach). **In them will be (Maidens), chaste, restraining their glances, whom no man or Jinn before them has touched.** Like unto Rubies and coral" (Q 55:54,56,58).

"Is there any Reward for Good - other than Good? **Then which of the favours of your Lord will ye deny?**" (Q 55: 60-61).

"And besides these two, there are two other Gardens, - In them (each) will be two Springs pouring forth water in continuous abundance. In them will be Fruits, and dates and pomegranates. **In them will be fair (Companions), good, beautiful. Companions restrained (as to their glances), in (goodly) pavilions. Whom no man or Jinn before them has touched**...Reclining on green Cushions and rich Carpets of beauty" (Q55:62, 66, 68, 70, 72, 74, 76).

"In it (heaven) are rivers of water incorruptible; rivers of milk of which the taste never changes; **rivers of wine, a joy to those who drink;** and rivers of honey pure and clear. In it there are for them all kinds of fruits; and Grace from their Lord" (Q 47:15).

"Then **which of the favours of your Lord will ye deny?** Blessed be the name of thy Lord, full of Majesty, Bounty and Honour" (Q 55: 77-78).

**Summary:** The above verses tell us that the heaven of Islam will be green and lush with all kinds of delicious fruits. It contains rivers of milk, honey, and wine, "a joy to those who drink." It will have an abundance of virgins ("whom no man or Jinn has touched"). Nothing will be denied to the one who attains Islam's heaven.

**Conclusion:** The heaven of Islam exists to indulge fleshly desires, nothing is denied.

## QUESTION THIRTEEN: DOES ISLAM ALLOW THE DRINKING OF ALCOHOLIC (FERMENTED) BEVERAGES?

**"O ye who believe! Intoxicants and gambling,** (dedication of) stones, and (divination by) arrows, are an abomination, of Satan's handwork: **eschew such (abomination),** that ye may prosper" (Q 5:90).

"...in it (heaven) are rivers of water incorruptible; rivers of milk of which the taste never changes; **rivers of wine, a joy to those who drink;** and rivers of honey pure and clear. In it there are for them all kinds of fruits; and Grace from their Lord" (Q 47:15).

"Truly the Righteous will be in Bliss. On Thrones (of Dignity) will they command a sight (of all things).Thou wilt recognise in their faces the beaming brightness of Bliss. **Their thirst will be slaked with Pure Wine sealed (to others)"** (Q 83:22-25).

**Summary:** The first verse commands the believers on earth to abstain from fermented drinks (intoxicants). The next two verses promise "rivers of wine" rewarded "to the righteous" in Islam's heaven.

**Conclusion:** Islam forbids the drinking of fermented beverages on earth, but provides it in abundance in Allah's heaven.

Now dear reader, let us look again at our original challenge. We looked to the Qur'an to see if we could find within it any incongruities, discrepancies, contradictions, or attributes that would seem to be unbecoming to a holy, righteous, and perfect God. We put the Qur'an to the test as suggested in the verse **"Do they not consider the Qur'an (with care)? Had it been from other than Allah, they would surely have found therein Much discrepancy"** (Q 4:82).

Here is a list of the conclusions:

1) There is a discrepancy as to the span of Allah's "Day".

2) The Qur'an gives contradictory messages regarding whether or not there is another mediator besides Allah.

3) The Qur'an presents contradictory messages regarding whether there will be many Muslims in heaven or only a few.

4) There is a discrepancy regarding exactly who will be present in heaven.

5) The Qur'an gives contradictory messages regarding whether to forgive and be lenient to unbelievers or to punish and subjugate them.

6) Allah allows adultery.

7) Allah swears by two cities.

8) Allah allows deception.

9) The Qur'an gives contradictory messages regarding methods (peaceful verses violent) in converting unbelievers. The majority of verses favor violence.

10) The Qur'an gives contradictory accounts regarding Pharaoh's outcome.

11) Allah's word is not pure. It changes as it caters to Muhammad's whims.

12) The heaven of Islam exists to indulge fleshly desires, nothing is denied.

13) Islam forbids the drinking of fermented beverages on earth, but provides it in abundance in Allah's heaven.

Now let us answer the question: Have we found any discrepancies, incongruities, contradictions, or attributes within the Qur'an that would be unbecoming to a perfect, and holy God? Sadly, dear reader, our only answer is yes.

## WHERE IS THE WITNESS?

Now dear reader, I would like to draw your attention to a central problem with Muhammad's claim to be a prophet from God. In the Middle Eastern culture, it is very important for there to be a second or third witness before making a judgment on any issue. Here are a few examples from the Qur'an, "O ye who believe... call to witness, from among your men, two witnesses. And if two men be not (at hand) then a man and two women, of such as ye approve as witnesses... And the witnesses must not refuse when they are summoned" (Q 2: 282). "And those who launch a charge against chaste women, and produce not four witnesses (to support their allegations), - flog them with eighty stripes; and reject their evidence ever after" (Q 24:4).

We have the same instruction from Moses in the Torah. We read, **"At the mouth of two witnesses, or three witnesses, shall he that is worthy of death be put to death; (but) at the mouth of one witness he shall not be put to death."** (Deuteronomy 17:6). Both the Qur'an and the Bible make it clear that no judgment is to be made on any issue without the testimony of more than one witness.

So, dear reader, where is the witness for Muhammad's claims to be a prophet from God? All the other prophets came to us with witnesses to confirm their messages. When Moses brought us the Torah, his message was confirmed by many miracles. When Jesus brought us the Injil (gospel), his message was confirmed by miracles, healings, signs and wonders. Muhammad has no witness other than himself. He claims that the miracle is the Qur'an. But we have just determined that the Qur'an is full of errors. So if his only witness is flawed then he has no witness at all.

So we must ask: who is the god of the Qur'an, and is Muhammad really a prophet? Let us take a look to see what the Bible has to say about this.

## DETERMINING IF A PROPHET IS FROM GOD

There are several tests given by God to determine if a prophet is truly from God. We cannot simply assume that someone who says he has had a revelation from God is a prophet. The Bible tells us to "**…test the spirits, whether they are of God; because many false prophets have gone out into the world**" (1 John 4:1). We are also told that, "**…For Satan transforms himself into an angel of light**" and that, "**the devil walks about like a roaring lion, seeking whom he may devour**" (2 Corinthians 11:15 and 1 Peter 5:8).

You see, dear reader, God loves us and He does not want us to be deceived. He has given us the Bible as a guide book for Salvation. If we let an imposter deceive us we will be led away from the truth of Scripture and the only One who can save us.

The first way we can guard ourselves from deception is to read the Scriptures and understand its message. If you search earnestly, asking the true God of heaven to help you understand the Scriptures, He will indeed. God promises us, "**…You will seek the LORD your God, and you will find Him if you seek Him with all your heart and with all your soul**" (Deuteronomy 4:29).

Another point I want to emphasize is the purity of the Bible. It is a document that was written and compiled over a period of roughly sixteen hundred years by forty different authors yet its message is entirely consistent and its judgments morally correct. We are told, "**Prophecy (Scripture) never came by the will of man, but holy men of God spoke as they were moved by the Holy Spirit**" (2 Peter 1:21). There are no discrepancies within the pages of the Bible (both the Old and New Testaments) because its author is the one true God.

Therefore, if someone claims to be a prophet, his message

must be consistent with Scripture. If his message is not consistent with Scripture we automatically know that he is not a prophet from God.

There are other ways that the Bible gives us to determine whether or not a prophet is from God. I will list some of them for you here. As you read through these I urge you to take the opportunity to see if Muhammad meets the test of a prophet from the Bible's standpoint.

### 1) The prophet's message must be entirely consistent with Scripture.

We have just discussed this in the preceding paragraphs. To summarize, the prophet's message cannot contradict what has been communicated to us in the Old and New Testaments.

### 2) A prophet cannot be assumed to be a prophet just because he claims to have had a vision or revelation from God.

The Bible tells us, "Let no one cheat you of your reward, taking delight in false humility and worship of angels, intruding into those things which he has not seen, vainly puffed up by his fleshly mind" (Colossians 2:18). "...Do not listen to the words of prophets who prophesy to you. They make you worthless; They speak a vision of their own heart, Not from the mouth of the LORD" (Jeremiah 23:16-17).

### 3) A prophet cannot be sly, tricky, or deceptive.

We read, "Beware of false prophets, who come to you in sheep's clothing, but inwardly are ravenous wolves. You will know them by their fruits...a good tree cannot bear bad fruit, nor can a bad tree bear good fruit" (Matthew 7: 15-16, 18).

## 4) If a prophet performs a miracle, it must be determined if the miracle is from God or from Satan.

The Bible warns us that Satan has the power to perform miracles and will perform them in order to deceive us. Consider the story of Moses and Pharaoh. Even Pharaoh's magicians were able to duplicate some of the miracles that Moses and Aaron performed. (Exodus, chapters 7-12) But their miracles were not from God, they were from Satan!

Here is another warning: "**If there arises among you a prophet or a dreamer of dreams, and he gives you a sign or a wonder, and the sign or the wonder comes to pass, of which he spoke to you, saying, 'Let us go after other gods' – which you have not known – 'and let us serve them,' you shall not listen to the words of that prophet or that dreamer of dreams, for the LORD your God is testing you...**" (Deuteronomy 13:1-3).

## 5) A prophet cannot mix together truth and error and cannot twist Scripture.

In the four gospels we read an account where the Spirit of God takes Jesus to a high mountain. Jesus fasts forty days. Towards the end of the forty days, Satan takes Jesus to the holy city, to the highest point of the temple. Then he tempts Him by quoting Scripture saying, "**...If you are the Son of God, throw Yourself down. For it is written: 'He shall give His angels charge over you' and, 'In their hands they shall bear you up, Lest you dash your foot against a stone**" (Matthew 4:6). Note that Satan is using a direct quote from Scripture (Psalm 91:11-12)! He is using the truth of Scripture in a twisted way to tempt Jesus.

Jesus answered saying, "**It is written again, 'You shall not tempt the LORD your God'**" (Matthew 4:7). Jesus answered Satan also by quoting Scripture (Deuteronomy 6:16) but this time by using it in its correct context! So we see here that Satan will use Scripture in an incorrect way to try and trick us! We in turn must know how to use Scripture correctly so that we will not be deceived!

## 6) A prophet cannot add words to the prophecies regarding the second coming of Jesus.

**"For I testify to everyone who hears the words of the prophecy of this book: If anyone adds to these things, God will add to him the plagues that are written in this book"** (Revelation 22:18).

Islam espouses an eschatology that is contrary to the eschatology of Scripture. If you are a Muslim who is familiar with the prophecies of Muhammad concerning the Mahdi, you know this. This is an example of adding words to the prophecies of Scripture. Unfortunately those who follow Islam's eschatology will find themselves on the wrong side of the end times battle and will suffer the consequences. Let this be a warning, dear reader!

## 7) A prophet cannot preach a different gospel.

We read, **"But even if we, or an angel from heaven, preach any other gospel to you that what we have preached to you, let him be accursed"** (Galatians 1: 8). This brings us back to point number one where the message of Scripture must be consistent. **Jesus is the message of Scripture**. He is the promised Messiah and the fulfillment of the Law and the Prophets. He is the message of salvation for all mankind. Again we read, **"Nor is there salvation in any other, for there is no other name under heaven given among men by which we must be saved"** (Acts 4:12). Islam cannot save us. Only Jesus can save us!!

My dear reader, did you take the time to see if Muhammad meets the Bible's criteria for a true prophet of God? In every instance Muhammad fails the Bible's criteria. Muhammad was not a prophet from God. He was deceived by Satan masquerading as an angel of light. We know from the Hadith that even Muhammad was suspicious of his visions and feared that they were from demons. On several occasions he even tried to kill himself (Bukhari part 6 page 2561). Unfortunately, in his great deception, many people of the Middle East and the world have been led astray.

Oh, I pray for you dear reader, that you will not be swallowed into Satan's trap. Please heed the Bible's warning so that you will escape the judgment that is coming upon all those who allow themselves to be deceived! Let the God of Scripture save you. He loves you dearly and desires to save you from the devil's clutches.

*"You shall not add to the word which I command you, nor take from it, that you may keep the commandments of the LORD your God which I command you."*

*Deuteronomy 4:2*

# 28

# No Alteration to the Word of Allah

"Do they not consider the Qur'an (with care)? Had it been from other Than Allah, they would surely have found therein Much discrepancy." (Q 4:82) Thanks be to the Lord, who has given us the ability to speak and to use the gift of thinking — which has distinguished us from all other forms of life. Upon accepting the Lord's ways and guidance, the rewards are very great, and are capped with the promise of an everlasting heaven. There will be much blessing and happiness, for Allah has said: "For those who follow the Faith there will be abundant rewards beyond anything imagined, beyond anything seen or heard before." Let us all hope to be among those fortunate ones.

The Lord who gave us a sound mind and right ideas will also lead and guide us to see the light and the truth which will lead us to safety. The Lord causes our hand to be extended for our salvation.

## TORAH

The Mighty God makes this pronouncement:

**"You shall not add to the word which I command you, nor take away from it..."** (Deuteronomy 4:2).

And at the conclusion of the illustrious Injil, we read this harsh warning;

**"For I testify to everyone who hears the words of the prophecy of this book: If anyone adds to these things, God will add to him the plagues that are written in this book; and if anyone takes away from the words of the book of this prophecy, God shall take away his part from the Book of Life, from the holy city, and from the things which are written in this book"** (Revelation 22:18-19).

After all these firm orders, should any faithful person challenge or change any of the Lord's words?

It has been thought by most Muslims that the Bible (the Torah, Zabur (Psalm), and the gospel **("Injil")** has been subjected to change at various times, either by adding something to it or taking something from it. Over the years, these thinkers have tried various means and methods to strengthen their position, but they have never really been able to establish sound proof. By failing to do so, they have lost any grounds to their claims.

My Muslim brother, it is too bad that some people even now are claiming that the Bible (Torah, Zabur and the gospel **"Injil"**) has been subjected to changes that contradict not only the (original) Bible, but also the Qur'an. It is unfortunate, because the Qur'an bears witness to the Bible, that the Bible is indeed the words of Allah, given by the good Lord to be light, guidance and mercy. The Bible is indeed the words of Allah, that will never be changed or ever subjected to challenge. The Qur'an testifies to this fact, that there can be no changes to Allah's words.

The evidence supporting the accuracy of the Bible is beyond any shadow of doubt. The Qur'an provides evidence, my Muslim brother that testifies to the fact that the Torah is a book given from the Lord to our master Moses to be guidance and mercy for the world.

**"It was We (Allah) who revealed the Law (to Moses): therein was Guidance and Light"** (Q 5: 47).

It is clear that the Torah is given to us from the Lord.

**"Say: 'Who then sent down the Book which Moses brought?--a Light and Guidance to man'"** (Q 6: 91).

Clearly, this is evidence that the Torah is absolutely given to us from the Lord:

**"We gave Moses the Book and followed him up"** (Q 2: 87).

We shall also note here that the Torah given to Moses by Allah is referred to as "the Book":

**"And remember We gave Moses the Scripture and the Criterion (between right and wrong): there was a chance for you to be guided aright"** (Q 2: 53).

There is here also an indication of the fact that the Torah was given to Moses (the book and the dividing line). Al-Bidawi says in his explanation (he is among the best to explain) that the dividing line means that the Torah combined the meaning of a book that put a clear distinction between right and wrong.

**"In the past We granted to Moses and Aaron the Criterion (for judgment) and a Light and a Message for those who would do right"** (Q 21: 48).

Al-Bidawi said in his explanation, also, that the Torah is a light to clear the way through despair and ignorance, to lead the people to the truth that will save them.

SUMMARY: It is clear to us now, my Muslim brother, following all this explanation, that the Torah is a book given to Moses by the Lord as guidance, light and mercy to the world. As a result, since the Torah is given by Allah, (the Qur'an bears witness to this), this makes the Torah the Word of Allah.

## ZABUR

Now to you, my Muslim brother, here are the Qur'an's words which testify that the Zabur (Psalms)was given to the prophet David:

_**"We did bestow on some prophets more (and other) gifts than on others; and we gave to David (the gift of) the Psalms"** (Q 17: 55).

**"Before this We wrote in the Psalms, after the message (given to Moses): 'My servants, the righteous, shall inherit the earth'"** (Q 21: 105).

SUMMARY: It is now clear to you, my Muslim brother, that the mighty Lord has given the Zabur to David. Again, as a result, since the Zabur also is given by Allah to David, (the Qur'an bears witness to this), this makes the Zabur also the Word of Allah.

## INJIL

Now, my Muslim brother, the fact is also clear that the Injil, (gospel) too, was given from Allah to our Master Issa the Messiah to be a light, guide and example to the Lord's fearing people.

**"Let the People of the Gospel (Injil) judge by what God hath revealed therein"** (Q 5: 50).

In this is an explanation of the fact that everything in the Injil is given by the Lord.

**"It is He who sent down to thee (step by step), in truth, the Book, confirming what went before it; and He sent down the Law (of Moses) and the Gospel (of Jesus) before this, as a guide to mankind, and he sent down the Criterion (between right and wrong)"** (Q 3: 3).

From this, it is clear that the Injil is given by the Lord to guide all the world, as also the Qur'an called (the Torah and the Injil) the dividing line. You will also note here the equality between the Qur'an, the Injil and the Torah.

**"Ye People of the Book! Why dispute ye about Abraham, when the Law and the Gospel were not revealed till after him"** (Q 3: 65)?

You can see from this verse how clear it is that the Torah and the Injil both were given by Allah.

**"And We caused Jesus, son of Mary, to follow in their footsteps, confirming that which was (revealed) before him, and We bestowed on him the Gospel wherein is Guidance and a Light, confirming that which was (revealed) before it in Torah — a guidance and an admonition unto those who ward off (evil)"** (Q 5: 49).

Again, you will note that the Injil was given to our Master

Issa also to be a guide and light.

**"Then, in their wake, We followed them up with (others of) Our apostles: We sent after them Jesus, the son of Mary, and bestowed on him the Gospel: and we ordained in the hearts of those who followed him Compassion and Mercy"** (Q 57: 27).

Yet one more time the Qur'an reassures us that the Injil was given by Allah to our Master Issa.

SUMMARY: From all this it is clear to both of us, my Muslim brother, that the Injil was given from the mighty Allah to our master Issa as a Guide and a Light to the world. Now since the Injil is the Book given by Allah, (the Qur'an bears witness to this), then the Injil is the word of Allah.

## HOLY BIBLE

My Muslim brother, here you will also find more evidence as to the authenticity of the Holy Bible (the Torah, Zabur and the Injil) in all its three parts.

**"And before thee also the apostles We sent were but men, to whom We granted inspiration: if ye realize this not, ask of those who possess the Message"** (Q 21: 7).

**"Thus doth (He) send inspiration to thee as (He did) to those before thee — God, exalted in Power, full of Wisdom"** (Q 42: 3).

From these two messages of the Lord it is clear to us as Muslims:

1. All the prophecy from Allah which was given to those

men of God who were before Muhammad was indeed given to them by the Lord. You will note the word before your Muhammad, you will also note the word given to your Muhammad.

2. Since Moses and David are among the famous prophets who lived before Muhammad, all their books were given by the Lord. And since Moses preached the Torah, David the Zabur, and Issa the Bible, these three books, therefore, were given to them by Allah.

3. The word given means that all that was given to them were the words of Allah; therefore, the Torah, Zabur and the Injil are the words of Allah.

**"We (Allah) have sent thee Inspiration, as We sent it to Noah and the Messengers after him: We sent Inspiration to Abraham, Isma'il, Isaac, Jacob and the Tribes, to Jesus, Job, Jonah, Aaron, and Solomon, and to David We gave the Psalms"** (Q 4: 163).

From this you will come to these conclusions:

(A) The words that descended from Allah to Muhammad were the same as those to Noah and the other prophets that followed him (note the word given to your Muhammad).

(B) Since Moses, David and Issa all came after Noah, all their teachings were given to them by the Lord. Also, all the books (the Torah, Zabur and Injil) were given by the Lord and, according to Islam, these were the words of Allah that were given to Moses, David and Issa.

SUMMARY: From all this, it is clear to us as Muslims that the Qur'an firmly declares the Holy Bible (the Torah, Zabur and the

Injil) to be the same given by the mighty Allah (referring back to Q 42: 3, Q 21: 7, and Q 4: 163).

# WHO GAVE US THE BOOK?

My Muslim brother, here are the titles of the Torah and the Injil as they are mentioned in the Qur'an:

### 1. The Qur'an gives the title "The Book" to the Torah and the Injil.

**"Say: 'O People of the Book! Ye have no ground to stand upon unless ye stand fast by the Law, the Gospel, and all the revelation that has come to you from your Lord'"** (Q 5: 71).

**"And dispute ye not with the People of the Book, except with means better (than mere disputation)..."** (Q 29: 46).

**"O ye People of the Book! Believe in what We have (now) revealed, confirming what was (already) with you..."** (Q 4: 47).

**"The People of the Book ask thee to cause a book to descend to them from Heaven..."** (Q 4:153).

From this you will note that the Qur'an clearly gives the title "The Book" to the Torah and the Injil. This is evidenced in that the Qur'an gives the Jews and Christians the title "People of the Book." This expression is repeated 20 times in the Qur'an.

### 2. The Qur'an gives the name "Al-Zikr" (Message of God) to the Torah and the Injil.

**"Before thee, also, the apostles We sent were but men, to whom We granted inspiration: If ye realize this not, ask of those who possess the Message"** (Q 21:7).

This citation is mentioned in the explanation of Al-Galaleen (page 357), concluding that the Qur'an gives the title "Al-Zikr" to the Torah and Injil.

SUMMARY: The titles "The Book" and "Al-Zikr" are titles the Qur'an uses to refer to itself. Since the Qur'an gives the Holy Bible the same name it gives itself, here is proof that the Torah and the Injil are given by the mighty Lord:

"It is He Who sent down to thee (step by step), in truth, the Book, confirming what went before it; and He sent down the Law (of Moses) and the Gospel (Of Jesus) before this, as a guide to mankind" (Q3: 3).

All of the above shows us clearly that the Qur'an ascribes guidance, light, mercy and revelation to the Torah and the Injil; the Qur'an then assures us that both the Torah and the Injil were given to us by the mighty Lord.

## FACTS FROM THE QUR'AN

1. The Torah, Zabur and Inji, are all heavenly books given to us by the mighty Lord (Q 5: 46, Q 17: 55; Q 3: 3).

2. The Torah, Zabur and Injil (gospel) are equal to the Qur'an (Q 42: 3; Q 21: 7; Q 4: 163).

3. The Qur'an has the same titles as the Torah and Injil ("The Book" and "Al- Zikr": see Q 5: 28: Q 21: 7).

4. The Qur'an describes both the Torah and the Bible as books fit to belong to the mighty Lord (Q 5:46,47, Q 3: 3).

From all of the above, you, my Muslim brother, will see clearly that the Qur'an states that the Holy Bible

<u>(the Torah, Zabur and Injil), is the Word of the Mighty Lord.</u>

Perhaps you may admit, after all, that the Holy Bible (the Torah, Zabur and Injil) is the word of the Mighty Lord, because the Qur'an testifies to this fact. But you may say that it was subjected to changes later in time. Then again, you may think, as some of our Muslim brothers do, that the Torah is a book given by the Lord because the Qur'an testifies to this fact, but that the Torah was subjected to changes after that time for the same reason Allah gave our Master Issa, the son of Mary, the Injil. However, these also have said that the Injil has also likewise been subjected to change, and that is why Allah sent the Qur'an to be the last chapter of His revelation.

Let me say to you, my Muslim brother, that the Qur'an itself testifies to the fact that there were no changes at all in any of Allah's words after they were given by him to Moses, David and Issa.

**"We (Allah) have, without doubt, sent down the Message: and We will assuredly guard it (from corruption)"** (Q 15: 9).

This citation shows clearly that the Torah and the Injil are both given by Allah and have been preserved without any alteration at all. You may think, my Muslim brother, that the Qur'an is meant to be the Holy Book (Al-Zikr) and not the Torah and Injil. But remember that it was the Qur'an itself that gave the two books the title "Al-Zikr."

**"Before this We (Allah) wrote in the Psalms, after the Message (given to Moses): 'My servants, the righteous, shall inherit the earth.'"** (Q 21: 105)

It is clear to you now that the Holy Book (Al-Zikr) means the Torah and not the Qur'an, the proof of which is the fact that the Zabur came after the Torah, not after the Qur'an.

**"Before thee, also, the apostles We (Allah) sent were but men, to whom We granted inspiration: If ye realize this not, ask of those who possess the Message."** (Q 21: 7)

Experts among whom are Al-Galaleen (page 357) and Ibn Kathir (page 502) hold the opinion that the people mentioned in Al-Zikr are the Jews and the Christians. Now you will agree with me, my Muslim brother, that both the Torah and the Injil are given by Allah and both have been preserved without any alteration at all.

Summary: We both shall note clearly that the Qur'an bears witness to the fact that there have been no changes to the words of Allah and that the Bible — the Torah, Zabur and Injil — is the word of Allah as we have already proven with support from various passages in the Qur'an.

Conclusion: The words of Allah given in the Bible have remained the same without any alteration, as every knowledgeable Muslim should know from the Qur'an. Therefore, my Muslim brother, when you still say that the Bible (the Torah, Zabur and Injil) has been subjected to change, you are saying the following:

1. The Qur'an is inaccurate: you see clearly that the Qur'an states the words of Allah never change, and yet you maintain that the Holy Bible was subjected to change.

2. Allah is underestimated because you infer that He was unable to preserve His words from change, even though the Qur'an has testified that there will be no change to the words of Allah.

3. The Qur'an was subjected to change: If the

Holy Bible (the Torah, Zabur and Injil) has ever been subjected to change, can you imagine what would happen to the Qur'an?

## WHEN THE CHANGE HAPPENED?

Let me ask you a question, my Muslim brother. If the Holy Bible was, in fact, subjected to changes, when do you think that this happened? Was it before or after the coming of Islam? If you think that the changes occurred prior to Islam, how is it that the Qur'an bears witness to and praises both the Torah and the Injil? Instead of any attack by the Qur'an on the Torah and Injil, there is nothing but praises and compliments. My Muslim brother, we all can see clearly that only a person who is not familiar with the Qur'an would think so, because there has been so much evidence to prove that the Holy Bible was in existence before and after the coming of Islam and has remained so without any alteration.

**"But why do they come to thee for judgment when they have the Torah, wherein Allah hath delivered judgment"** (Q 5: 46).

You will find that there was an interesting event which took place in the time of the prophet Muhammad (see Ibn Kathir, pages 517-518). It is told that a group of Jews came to the prophet Muhammad, asking him to determine the fate of a man and woman who had committed adultery. The prophet told them to consult the Torah. When they tried to hide the part stating that capital punishment (by stoning) was the punishment for the offense, the prophet Muhammad knew what they were after and he ordered them to apply the capital punishment. The man and the woman were, therefore, stoned to death. This will serve as evidence to you, my Muslim brother, that the Torah had never been subjected to change.

**"Say: 'O People of the Book!  Ye have no ground to stand upon unless ye stand fast by the Law, the Gospel, and all revelation that has**

**come to you from your Lord'"** (Q 5: 71).

You will note that both the Torah and the Injil were in existence during the same period as the Qur'an, without any changes. Otherwise, the Qur'an would never ask both the Jews and Christians to follow the words and rules of the Torah and Injil respectively.[15]

**"Let the People of the Gospel judge by what God hath revealed therein. If any do fail to judge by (the light of) what God hath revealed, they are (no better than) those who rebel"** (Q 5: 50).

Again you will note that the Qur'an ordered the Christians to apply the rules of the Bible to their lives. It would be impossible for the Qur'an to do so if the Bible had been subjected to any kind of alteration at any given time.[16]

**"Hast thou not seen how those who have received the Scripture invoke the Scripture of Allah (in their disputes) that it may judge between them: then a faction of them turn away, being opposed (to it)?"** (Q 3: 23).

The important question here, my Muslim brothers, is: How could it be possible for the Qur'an to ask the Jews to go back to the Torah, as a reference to their rules? You have to agree with me that this would be impossible if the Torah had been subjected to any changes and remained so during the Islamic period.

The very fact that the Qur'an calls the Jews and the Christians to follow exactly the rules of the Torah and Injil, respectively, is another proof of the fact that the Torah and Injil were never subjected to change. The historian Al-Bidawi stated that the prophet Muhammad was fond of the Hebrew schools where the Torah was taught. When someone asked him (Naiem ben 'Amr) about which Faith he was devoted to, his answer was, "I am devoted to Abraham and the Torah."

"O ye People of the Book! Believe in what We (Allah) have revealed, confirming that which ye possess" (Q 4: 47).

Herein you will note that Ibn Kathir came to the same understanding that the Qur'an supports both the Torah and the Injil.

"And believe in what I (Allah)reveal, confirming the revelation which is with you" (Q 2: 41).

"Then an Apostle comes to you, confirming what is with you." (Q 3: 81)

"And when there comes to them a Book from God, confirming what is with them..." (Q 2: 89).

"And when it is said to them, "Believe in what God hath sent down." they say, "We believe in what was sent down to us": yet they reject all besides, even though it is the Truth confirming that which they possess" (Q 2: 91).

Again in Ibn Kathir, page 89, you will find that the Qur'an clearly testifies to the accuracy and authenticity of the Torah and Injil, which would not be possible if they had been subjected to any change.

There are also numerous explanations by Ibn Kathir which provide a list of events reflecting the prophet Muhammad's great feeling of support and admiration for the Torah and Injil during the period of time when the prophet Muhammad was on earth.

"And if you (Muhammad) are in doubt concerning that which We (Allah) have revealed unto thee, then ask those who have been reading the Book (that was) before thee." (Q 10: 94)

Also, Al-Bidawi came to the same conclusion when the Qur'an stated: "If you are in doubt [referring to the prophet Muhammad], ask those before you [meaning the Jews and the Christians]." We came to the same conclusion that both the Torah and Injil were very familiar to the prophet Muhammad and were both safe from any alteration. I hope now, my Muslim brother, that you agree with me that the Torah and Injil were never ever subjected to any change of any kind at any time before, during or after the coming of Islam.

## THE CONCLUSION OF THIS RESEARCH

Both the Torah and Injil were in existence during the time when the Qur'an was given to the prophet Muhammad and stayed as such without any alteration. The proof of this is as follows:

1. The Muslim prophet (Muhammad) told the Jews to go back to the Torah to be a referee between both of them (Q 3: 23). It is obvious that the Prophet would never have done so if the Torah had been subjected to change.

2. The Qur'an shows astonishment at the Jewish people's behavior when they attempted to use the Qur'an as a referee, in light of the fact that they did not even believe in the Qur'an. You will note here that because the Torah was an acceptable prophecy in the eyes of the prophet Muhammad, he was astonished that they did not use their Torah as a rule and as guidance (Q 5: 47-52).

3. Since the prophet of Islam told the people of the Injil (i.e., the Christians) to believe in everything that came in the Injil and to follow it (Q 5: 52), it is obvious that the Muslim prophet could never have told the Christian people so if the Injil was ever subjected to any change. This is also a proof of the unchanged existence of the Injil during the time of Islam.

4. When the Muslim prophet insisted that both the Jews and the Christians hold closely to the Torah and Injil in regard to the rules that came in both books (see Q 5: 47-52), do you think for a moment that the prophet Muhammad would do so if the Torah or Injil had been subjected to any change?

5. It is a fact that the Qur'an bears witness to the authenticity and accuracy of both the Torah and the Injil (see Q 3: 81; Q 5: 47-52; Q 4: 47, and Q 2: 89-91).

6. The Qur'an advised the Muslim prophet to seek assistance from the people who read the Torah and Injil whenever he was in doubt about any fundamental religious matters (when you are in doubt, Muhammad). You would not suggest for a moment, would you, that Allah would refer his Prophet Muhammad to the Torah and Injil if they had ever been subjected to any alteration?

7. The Qur'an itself demands from the Jews and the Christians to have full faith in the Torah and Injil.

**"O ye who believe! Believe in God and His Apostle, and the Scripture which He hath revealed unto His Apostle and the Scripture which He revealed to those in earlier times. Any who denieth God, His angels, His Books, His Apostles, and the Day of Judgment, hath gone far, far astray"** (Q 4: 136).

It does not make any sense, my Muslim brother, that the Quran would ask Muslims to have faith in the Bible that came before the Qur'an if it were not a true record. This is full proof of the accuracy of the Bible, for the Qur'an would never have asked Muslims to do so if the Bible had ever been subjected to change.

It is clear to you now, my Muslim brother, after all this research and all this evidence from the Qur'an, that it is beyond any shadow of a doubt that both the Torah and Injil were kept safe from any wrongdoing during the time of the Qur'an. But you may think, my Muslim brother, that in spite of the fact that the Torah and Injil were kept safe from any wrongdoing during the time of the Qur'an (because the Qur'an testifies to this fact), the damage occurred at a later time. Let me tell you, my Muslim brother, that the Qur'an itself rejects this idea because of the following facts:

1. In Qur'an 5: 51, it says:

**"And unto thee have We (Allah) revealed the scripture with the truth, confirming whatever scripture was before it and a watcher over it."**

The meaning of "watcher over it" is that scripture will always be safe from any change or wrongdoing. Therefore, suggesting that any change took place after the Qur'an was revealed is to imply that the Qur'an failed in its job as a watcher over the Torah and Injil. In other words, if the Torah and Injil were subjected to change after the Qur'an, this would imply that the people of the Qur'an failed even to keep one or more copies of the Torah and Injil intact as a watcher over them.

When the Christians found that the Torah contained a lot of scriptures about Jesus, they made themselves watchers over the Torah and spread it throughout the world. It is estimated that the Torah was translated into every language known to man. Why then did Muslims not do the same thing, since they believed that the Torah and Injil contained many signs referring to the Qur'an and the Prophet Muhammad?

2. Since we have already established the fact that the Torah and Injil were kept safe from any changes in the Qur'an's time, this will lead us to the following conclusions:

A. The true Christians — in the time of the Qur'an — always kept a copy of the Torah because it contained many scriptures about Jesus and the Injil. Moreover, Jesus himself bore witness to the rightfulness of the Torah. It is related in the Qur'an also: **"We caused Jesus, son of Mary, to follow in their footsteps, confirming that which was revealed before him, and which we bestowed on him, the gospel wherein is guidance and a light confirming that which was revealed before it in the Torah"** (Q 5: 49). In this case, if the Jews tried to change the Torah, the Christians would have discovered the changes immediately because they kept the original copy of the Torah.

B. By the same logic, if the Christians had wanted to change the Torah, the Jews would have stopped them immediately by showing the original copy of the Torah.

C. Likewise, if the Jews had made an attempt to change the Injil, the Christians would have stopped them by showing the original copy of the Injil.

3. As a matter of fact, Islam came 570 years after Christianity. During this pre-Islamic period, Christianity was spread all over the world, including the Arab world, North Africa, Iran, India, and Europe. This made it impossible for people in any of these countries to change the Injil at the same time without someone objecting to the error.

4. The mere fact that these countries have different languages makes it too difficult to change the Injil.

5. And now, my Muslim brother, we must ask ourselves where and when the change was made and who made the change? There is no one who can come up with a single name of any historian, Jew or Christian, to confirm that such an event ever took place. Moreover, if any alteration ever did take place with the approval of both the Jews and the Christians, this means that there is a contradiction to what the Qur'an has testified — namely, that there is no one who can change Allah's words:

**"And recite that which has been revealed to thee of the Book of the Lord: There is none who can change His words"** (Q 18: 27).

There is no doubt that the word "Book" in the above scripture refers to the Qur'an, but the expression "His words" refers to the Holy Bible (Torah, Zabur and Injil). All these books are Allah's words and we believe that none can alter His words.

**"There is no alteration to the words of Allah"** (Q 10: 64).

**"There is none that can alter the words of God"** (Q 6: 34).

# RECAP

1. The Bible (Torah, Zabur and Injil) is the word of Allah given by Him to His messengers before you. The Gospel (Injil) was Guidance, Light and Mercy to the world.

2. The Qur'an establishes equality between itself and the Bible (Torah, Zabur and Injil) due to the fact that all these Books were given by Allah to His messengers before you.

3. The Qur'an gave itself the same title as it did the Holy Bible, "the Book."

4. The words of Allah that were given by Him to his messengers remained the same and have never been subjected to any change.

**"We have, without doubt, sent down the Message: and We will assuredly guard it (from corruption)"** (Q 15: 9).

5. The Holy Bible was in existence during the same period in which the Qur'an was revealed. The proof of this is that the prophet Muhammad demanded the Jews to bring the Torah to be a referee for the debate between them.

6. It is implausible to suggest that any of the Holy Books were subjected to any change due to the fact that the Torah and the Injil were spread throughout the world in different languages.

## MY DEAR MUSLIM BROTHER

All this research is supported by scriptures from the Qur'an and also supported by some of the most famous Muslim scholars, such as Ibn Kathir, Al-Badawi, Al-Galaleen and Al-Bukhari.

I have gone to such great lengths in order to make every true Muslim rest assured that this research was done in complete honesty and truth. I have been careful to use the Qur'an as the main source, in order to assure you that when you, my Muslim brother, are finished reading this research, you will have to agree with me that the Holy Bible (Torah, Zabur and Injil) has been preserved from any change or alteration. All these Books are Allah's words, and we believe that there are none who can change His words.

**"There is no alteration to the words of Allah"** (Q 10:64).

**"There is none that can alter the words of God"** (Q 6: 34).

**"We have, without doubt, sent down the Message: and We will assuredly guard it (from corruption)"** (Q 15: 9).

*"You watched while a stone was cut out without hands, which struck the image on its feet of iron and clay, and broke them in pieces. Then the iron, the clay, the bronze, the silver, and the gold were crushed together, and became like chaff from the summer threshing floors, the wind carried them away so that no trace of them was found. And the stone that struck the image became a great mountain and filled the whole earth."*

Daniel 2:34-35

# 29

# Islam and Nebuchadnezzar's Image

Finally, my dearest brothers and sisters we must ask a very serious question: where did Islam come from? We have already seen that Islam does not repair the human condition. We have seen in the previous chapters the many inconsistencies and contradictions within the Qur'an. We have also seen the vast differences between the lives of Muhammad and Christ. So how did Islam evolve to be such a predominant religion in the world?

My study of this subject has led me to believe that Muhammad took some truths from the Torah and the New Testament that he had heard from the Jews and Christians that were in Arabia at the time, and then mixed them with the imaginations and fleshly desires of his own mind. I also believe that the "revelations" he supposedly received were not from the angel Gabriel but, in fact, were from the fallen angel, Satan, whom the Bible describes as disguising himself as an "angel of light" (See 2 Corinthians 11:14). The Hadith tells us that

Muhammad was visited by evil spirits and was so tormented by them that he tried several times to throw himself over a high mountain.[17]

## THE IMAGE IN THE DREAM

One day, while I was sitting in an airplane on my way to do a TV recording, I asked the Lord with all my heart to show me how the prophet Muhammad came up with this deceptive religion and why it has entrapped so many of my people. As I was praying about this, God brought to my attention the story in the Bible where King Nebuchadnezzar has a troubling dream about an Image. We find a description of this image in the second chapter of the book of Daniel where Daniel recounts the dream for the King.

**"You, O king, were watching; and behold, a great image! This great image, whose splendor was excellent, stood before you; and its form was awesome. This image's head was of fine gold, its chest and arms of silver, its belly and thighs of bronze, its legs of iron, its feet partly of iron and partly of clay. You watched while a stone was cut out without hands, which struck the image on its feet of iron and clay, and broke them in pieces. Then the iron, the clay, the bronze, the silver, and the gold were crushed together, and became like chaff from the summer threshing floors; the wind carried them away so that no trace of them was found. And the stone that struck the image became a great mountain and filled the whole earth"** (Daniel 2:31-35).

God gave the dream of the statue to represent the successive kingdoms that were to dominate the world until the second coming of Christ. Babylon was the first of these world kingdoms as represented in the head of gold. This dream should have humbled Nebuchadnezzar moving him to worship God. But instead of giving glory to God, Nebuchadnezzar made an image of himself which he commanded his subjects to worship.

**"Nebuchadnezzar the king made an image of gold, whose height was sixty cubits and its width six cubits. He set it up in the plain of Dura, in the province of Babylon. And King Nebuchadnezzar sent word to gather together the satraps, the administrators, the governors, the counselors, the treasurers, the judges, the magistrates, and all the officials of the provinces, to come to the dedication of the image which King Nebuchadnezzar had set up.**

So... (they all) gathered together for the dedication of the image that King Nebuchadnezzar had set up; and they stood before the image that Nebuchadnezzar had set up. Then a herald cried aloud: 'To you it is commanded, O peoples, nations, and languages, that at the time you hear the sound of the horn, flute, harp, lyre, and psaltery, in symphony with all kinds of music, you shall fall down and worship the gold image that King Nebuchadnezzar has set up; and whoever does not fall down and worship shall be cast immediately into the midst of a burning fiery furnace'" (Daniel 3:1-6).

## THE IMAGE OF ISLAM

As I was thinking about the statue and its components (gold, silver, bronze, iron, clay), the realization came to me that this statue is also an illustration of Islam. Let us look at some curious parallels between the statue in Nebuchadnezzar's dream and the religion of Islam.

Islam is a mixture of ancient pagan religions along with elements found in Judaism and Christianity. The pure metals of gold and silver in the statue of Nebuchadnezzar's dream can be likened to the Jewish and Christian Scriptures. The bronze, iron, and clay can be likened to the pagan practices of ancient Arabia. All of these mixed together represent the whole statue which is likened to Islam.

We have already seen, in previous chapters, the verses in the Qur'an that contain some Biblical truths. Now let's look at the pagan elements of Islam.

## WORSHIP OF THE MOON

The first pagan element in Islam is the emphasis that is placed on the moon. We see this in the month of Ramadan which is dependent on the phases of the moon. We see this represented also in the flags of many Islamic nations with the depiction of the crescent moon. Worship of the moon has its origins in the pagan rites of the past, but its vestiges are still seen today in the fifth pillar of Islam which emphasizes pilgrimage to Mecca.

Let us look first at the origins of the word "Allah". Most people think that the word "Allah" is the Arabic term for the word "God". They believe that Allah is Islam's equivalent to the Christian and Jewish God. But this, in fact, is not the case.

Allah was known as a god in Arabia long before the inception of Islam. He was one of the well known pagan deities worshipped by the people of Quraysh which was the tribe Muhammad was born into. Muhammad's parents worshipped this pagan god, Allah, even adopting the name "Allah" as their surname. Muhammad's given name was, Muhammad Abd-Allah, which means, "Muhammad the servant of Allah."

At the time of Muhammad's birth, Allah was commonly known as the moon god. He was one of many Meccan deities.[18] Archeological evidence supports the fact that the moon god, Allah, was worshipped in pre-Islamic times. In fact, the pagan god Bel, of the ancient Babylonians, is thought to be the predecessor of Allah, the moon god of the Arabian Peninsula.[19] Muhammad was raised with the belief in these many deities, among which Allah was chief.

In the early stages of Islam everyone understood that the Allah of the Qur'an was the same pagan moon god of their ancestors. They also understood that Allah was distinct from the God of the Jews and the Christians. Muhammad kept the term Allah to refer to the Qur'an's deity because he knew his pagan followers would not object. His command to his pagan followers was that they were now to make Allah their only god as opposed to the rest of their deities. This is why the first pillar of Islam is the Al-Shahadah. This is the confession which states that, "There is no other god besides Allah." In reality this does not mean that "there is no other god but god" as is commonly thought. It means that "there is no other god but the moon god, Allah." Today, the origins of this term are not commonly known, not even to many learned Muslims.

## THE BLACK STONE

In Mecca, there is a famous meteorite know as the Black Stone. In pre-Islamic times it was believed to have fallen from the sky as a result of cosmic forces in the heavens. Beliefs in pagan deities surrounding this mysterious stone were passed down through the generations. By Muhammad's time, worship of this meteorite was firmly entrenched in the culture. The people were accustomed to worshipping it by bowing to it and kissing it in the hope receiving good fortune. The god Allah was known as the stone's chief overseer.

Muhammad did not abolish the practice of paying homage to this stone and its deity, Allah. He even performed it himself as an example to his followers. Al-Bukhari records a famous statement made by Umar Ibn al-Khattab the second successor after Muhammad. It says, "When 'Umar ibn al-Khattab reached the Black Stone, he kissed it and said, 'I know that you are a stone that does not hurt or benefit. If I had not seen the prophet (Muhammad) kiss you, I would have not kissed you.'"[20]

The Fifth Pillar of Islam that Muhammad established is the Hajj. The Hajj is the pilgrimage to Mecca where devout Muslims are instructed to circle (make rotation) around the Ka'ba. Muhammad also instituted the practice of praying towards Mecca where the Ka'ba resides. This was in direct contrast to the practice of the Jews and Christians living in Arabia at the time who would pray facing Jerusalem.

## WORSHIP OF LAT, UZZA, AND MANAT

Worship of the ancient gods Lat, Uzza, and Manat was practiced by the Jaahiliyyah ("ignorant ones") who existed centuries before Muhammad. Worship of these deities was carried out by the people of Quraysh and other Arabian pagan tribes. Muhammad did not denounce the worship of these deities. In fact, he continued in them. We read Muhammad's own words, "Have ye seen Lat, and 'Uzza, And another, the third (goddess), Manat? What! for you the male sex, and for Him, the female?" (Q 53:19-20).

When Muhammad was accused of worshipping these gods he recanted. He claimed that the devil had put these verses in his mouth, and that later Allah corrected him by providing "better verses". This is an example of what Islam calls the abrogation theory. The abrogation theory states that Allah adds or deletes verses from the Qur'an as he pleases.[21]

Here is how the Islamic scholar Jalalan summarizes the

account, "(The angel) Gabriel came to Muhammad and told him that Satan had thrust this verse to him…"[22] Another commentator, Ibn Hisham wrote, "Satan instilled (this verse) in his (Muhammad) recitation and he (Muhammad) acknowledged (Satan's) intervention. The infidels were overjoyed and said, 'He mentioned our idols with good words.'" Ibn Hisham goes on to say that the Angel Gabriel, on Allah's behalf, was sent to Muhammad, to rectify the matter. Allah, through the angel Gabriel, says, "I (Allah) did not bring to you these verses (about the idols)."[23]

## HEAVEN IN ISLAM

A false understanding of heaven is also evident in the Qur'an. Many of the elements of the Islamic heaven are similar to the elements of heaven described in the religions of ancient India.[24] Sheikh Al Sha'rawi a famous Egyptian Islamic scholar and leader said, "The apostle of god was asked, 'Will we have sexual intercourse in paradise?' He said, 'Yes, I swear by the One who holds my soul in His hand that it will be a vigorous intercourse, and as soon as the man departs from her (the houris) she will again become immaculate and virgin.'"[25]

## AN UNHOLY MIXTURE OF ELEMENTS

These religions and practices (Judaism, Christianity, and various varieties of paganism) were observed by the various tribes living in Arabia at the time of Muhammad. In order to win the favor of these tribes he concocted a mixture of them. This resulted in the Image of Islam, not unlike the statue in Nebuchadnezzar's dream with its mixture of pure (gold and silver) and impure (bronze, iron, clay) elements.

We can also make parallels between Nebuchadnezzar and Muhammad. Just as Nebuchadnezzar did not give glory to God but instead made an image to glorify himself, Muhammad did not heed the truth that he learned from the people of the Book but instead built a new religion and appointed himself its highest authority. Also, just as Nebuchadnezzar forced his subjects to worship him or suffer the consequences of a fiery end, Muhammad instituted the doctrines of Jihad (the sword) and the Jizya (tax paid by infidels) in order to conquer and subjugate all who tried to resist him.

The iron in the statue of Nebuchadnezzar's dream can be likened to the sword of Islam. Just as iron has been a key component used to fashion weaponry throughout history, so violence has been a key element in the doctrine of Islam with which to gain land, power, and control. Since the inception of Islam many nations and peoples have been slaughtered and overrun by its sword. Even to this very day the tentacles of Islam's iron fist continue to cause untold havoc and suffering around the world (Q 2:193).

Now dear reader, I would like to continue from the Book of Daniel. We left off where Nebuchadnezzar had set up the golden image commanding his subjects to worship it upon pain of fiery death. There were, however, some young men living in Babylon at the time, exiles of Judea, who would not heed the king's command.

"So at that time, when all the people heard the sound of the horn, flute, harp, and lyre, in symphony with all kinds of music, all the people, nations, and languages fell down and worshiped the gold image which King Nebuchadnezzar had set up.

Therefore at that time certain Chaldeans came forward and accused the Jews. They spoke and said to King Nebuchadnezzar, 'O king, live forever! You, O king, have made a decree that everyone who hears the sound of the horn, flute, harp, lyre, and psaltery, in symphony with all kinds of music, shall fall down and worship the gold image; and whoever does not fall down and worship shall be cast into the midst of a burning fiery furnace. There are certain Jews whom you have set over the affairs of the province of Babylon: Shadrach, Meshach, and Abed-Nego; these men, O king, have not paid due regard to you. They do not serve your gods or worship the gold image which you have set up.'

Then Nebuchadnezzar, in rage and fury, gave the command to bring Shadrach, Meshach, and Abed-Nego. So they brought these men before the king. Nebuchadnezzar spoke, saying to them, 'Is it true, Shadrach, Meshach, and Abed-Nego that you do not serve my gods or worship the gold image which I have set up? Now if you are ready at the time you hear the sound of the horn, flute, harp, lyre, and psaltery, in symphony with all kinds of music, and you fall down and worship the image which I have made, good! But if you do not worship, you shall be cast immediately into the midst of a burning fiery furnace. And who is the god who will deliver you from my hands?'

Shadrach, Meshach, and Abed-Nego answered and said to the king, 'O Nebuchadnezzar, we have no need to answer you in this matter. If that is the case, our God whom we serve is able to deliver us from the burning fiery furnace, and He will deliver us from your hand, O king. But if not, let it be known to you, O king, that we do not serve your gods, nor will we worship the gold image which you have set up.'

Then Nebuchadnezzar was full of fury, and the expression on his face changed toward Shadrach, Meshach, and Abed-Nego. He spoke and commanded that they heat the furnace seven times more than it was usually heated. And he commanded certain mighty men of valor who were in his army to bind Shadrach, Meshach, and Abed-Nego, and cast them into the burning fiery furnace.

> "...WE dO NOT SERVE YOUR GOds, NOR will WE WORSHip THE GOLD iMAGE WHICH yOU HAVE SET up."
>
> DANIEL 3:18

Then these men were bound in their coats, their trousers, their turbans, and their other garments, and were cast into the midst of the burning fiery furnace. Therefore, because the king's command was urgent, and the furnace exceedingly hot, the flame of the fire killed those men who took up Shadrach, Meshach, and Abed-Nego. And these three men, Shadrach, Meshach, and Abed-Nego, fell down bound into the midst of the burning fiery furnace.

Then King Nebuchadnezzar was astonished; and he rose in haste and spoke, saying to his counselors, 'Did we not cast three men bound into the midst of the fire?'

They answered and said to the king, 'True, O king.'

'Look!' he answered, 'I see four men loose, walking in the midst of the fire; and they are not hurt, and the form of the fourth is like the Son of God.' Then Nebuchadnezzar went near the mouth of the burning fiery furnace and spoke, saying, 'Shadrach, Meshach, and Abed-Nego, servants of the Most High God, come out, and come here.' Then Shadrach, Meshach, and Abed-Nego came from the midst of the fire.

And the satraps, administrators, governors, and the king's counselors gathered together, and they saw these men on whose bodies the fire had no power; the hair of their head was not singed nor were their garments affected, and the smell of fire was not on them.

Nebuchadnezzar spoke, saying, 'Blessed be the God of Shadrach, Meshach, and Abed-Nego, who sent His Angel and delivered His servants who trusted in Him, and they have frustrated the king's word, and yielded their bodies, that they should not serve nor worship any god except their own God!'" (Daniel 3:7-28).

This is a most beautiful story. God blessed these young men by sparing them from the fiery furnace because they courageously refused to bow down to the image. They were willing to die to honor the true and living God. Muslim converts to Christianity are like Shadrach, Meshach, and Abednego. They refuse to bow down to the image of Muhammad (Islam). They are willing, in the face of death and persecution, to stand courageously.

Beloved reader, do not be afraid to stand up to the image of Islam. Do not be afraid to confidently say, "Muhammad, I do not worship you and do not worship your god or the statue of Islam that you have set up. There is a God who is able to save me from your hand and all the ways of death and suffering. Even if He were not to save me from death or suffering in this life, dying for Christ is my gain" (See Philippians 1:21).

I am so thankful for all those who have escaped from the grip of Muhammad and now boldly, along with the apostle Paul, give the good confession, "But what things were gain to me, these I have counted loss for Christ. Yet indeed I also count all things loss for the excellence of the knowledge of Christ Jesus my Lord, for whom I have suffered the loss of all things, and count them as rubbish, that I may gain Christ" (Philippians 3:7-8).

## DESTRUCTION OF THE IMAGE

Beloved Muslim, I love you and wish with all my heart to free you from Islam. I wish to release you from bondage to this statue which Muhammad erected for his own glory and pride. Now let us return to the statue in Nebuchadnezzar's dream to see how the dream ends.

**"You, O king, were watching; and behold, a great image! This great image, whose splendor was excellent, stood before you; and its form was awesome. This image's head was of fine gold, its chest and arms of silver, its belly and thighs of bronze, its legs of iron, its feet partly of iron and partly of clay. You watched while a stone was cut out without hands, which struck the image on its feet of iron and clay, and broke them in pieces. Then the iron, the clay, the bronze, the silver, and the gold were crushed together, and became like chaff from the summer threshing floors; the wind carried them away so that no trace of them was found. And the stone that struck the image became a great mountain and filled the whole earth"** (Daniel 2:31-35).

Halleluiah! The statue has been finally crushed! But how did this happen? A Stone, not cut from human hands, struck the statue at its feet. This Stone, dear reader, is the Lord Jesus Christ! Let us examine this more closely, and may God give you clear insight as we look at this.

Notice first that this Stone was not cut or made by human hands. This indicates the final world kingdom will not be destroyed by human military force. It will be destroyed by Jesus coming with the armies of heaven (spiritual heavenly forces) as He returns to set up His kingdom. This is the huge mountain that fills the whole earth! (Revelation 19:14-20:5). The Bible describes Jesus Christ as being **"the chief cornerstone"** (1 Peter 2:6). He is the one who conquers, not through human effort, but by the Spirit of God.

All political kingdoms and false philosophies will be crushed at the Lord's second coming. Islam along with everything else that sets itself up against the true God will be turned to dust and thrown to the wind. Very soon we will see King Jesus coming to take His rightful throne. Halleluiah!

## WHOSE IMAGE WILL YOU BOW TO?

We are nearing the end of history as we know it. The Bible says, **"...the end of all things is at hand"** (1 Peter 4:7). Islam will crumble along with all the other false religions, philosophies, and world political systems. When Jesus returns He will cast out all the impurities of the world and set up His own glorious kingdom. The Bible tells us that He will be assisted by all those who have been redeemed by His blood and come out of Satan's dark trap ( Revelation 12:11). Already we see many millions all over the world being released from the trap of false religions, especially among those enslaved by the clutches of Islam.

Soon we will enter the Messianic Age when all of creation will live in great peace and joy along with our beloved Messiah and Savior. There will be no more struggles for political domination of one people group over another. There will be no more sin, sorrow or pain. The Bible tells us that even the animals will live in peace with one another. Everything will be set right as in the days before Adam was cast from the garden.

Here is a glimpse of what life will be like when Jesus returns to set all things right:

**"They shall not build and another inhabit; They shall not plant and another eat; For as the days of a tree, so shall be the days of My people, And My elect shall long enjoy the work of their hands. They shall not labor in vain, Nor bring forth children for trouble; For they shall be the descendants of the blessed of the LORD, And their offspring with them. 'It shall come to pass that before they call, I will answer; And while they are still speaking, I will hear. The wolf and the lamb shall feed together, The lion shall eat straw like the ox, And dust shall be the serpent's food. They shall not hurt nor destroy in all My holy mountain,' Says the LORD"** (Isaiah 65:22-25).

The question is whose side will you be on? Will it be on the side of Islam that is built of iron and clay? Or will it be on the side of the Stone "not cut from human hands?" Listen again to Abu Bakr's words, "Choose for yourself who you will worship. Whoever worships Muhammad worships a dead man, but whoever worships God is alive and will never die."[26] Muhammad's grave is in Saudi Arabia and still exists as a witness to his mortality. But Jesus is alive forever and ever! Will you bow to Muhammad's image that lies dead in the sands of the Arabian Desert or Jesus Christ the Living One?

## FINAL WORD

Do you remember Muhammad's words where he said that Islam started as an alien ("stranger") religion and that it will end the same way?[27] He did not realize how true his words were in saying this. Islam is a stranger religion. It is not the pure and undefiled religion of the true Lord and His Anointed One, the Christ.

Please, come to Christ, hide in his wounds and be cleansed by His blood. For He is the Momentous Sacrifice that takes away the sins of the world (See John 1:29). **"Nor is there salvation in any other, for there is no other name under heaven given among men by which we must be saved"** (Acts 4:12). Seek the Lord earnestly and He will be faithful to show you the way, the truth and the life. God is saying to you, **"…call upon Me and go and pray to Me, and I will listen to you. You will seek Me and find Me when you search for Me with all your heart. I will be found by you, says the LORD"** (Jeremiah 29:12-14).

I pray, dear reader, that you will receive eternal life through the blood of Issa, the Messiah, and that you will be present in His coming kingdom.

Dear Muslim,

If you have any questions or you would like to receive a free copy of the Bible in Arabic or any other language, please write to me at this address:

Open The Gates
P.O. Box 270333
San Diego, CA 92198

Publication@openthegates.org

I would be honored to send this as a gift to you.

Finally, dear brothers and sisters, I leave you in God's protection, love and mercy.

Sincerely,
Your brother,
Daniel Massieh

# Bibliography

Ali, Abdullah Yusuf. THE MEANING of THE Holy QUR'AN. ENGLISH EDITION, AMANA PUBLICATION, BELTSVILLE,MD (1996)

Al –Baidawi, COMENTARY ON THE QUR'AN. DAR Al KOTOB AL-IlmiYAH, BEIRUT, (1996)

Al-RAZI. TAFSIR-AL KABIR. Vol 3, DAR EHIA AL-TOURATH AL-ARABI, BEIRUT (1999)

Al SIRA AL-NABAWIA ABIN HISHAM by IBN MUHAMMAD ABDEL Al MALAK, PublisHED by

DAR Al BAIAN AL-ARABI (1425-2001 H)

Abi HANIFAH. AL-FIQH AL-AKBAR. DAR AL-KUTUB AL-ElMEYAH, BEIRUT (1979)

"AMERICAN TALIBAN," EVAN THOMAS NEWS WEEK (DECEMBER 17, 2001)

ENCYClopEDIA of RELIGION, (ED. Gibb), 1:406

ENCYClopEdiA of RELIGION, EDS. PAUL MEAGHER, THOMAS O'BRIAN, CONSUElA

ABERNE (WASHINGTON D. C.: CORPUS Pub.1979), 1:117

Encyclopedia of World Mythology and Legend, 1:61

History of Al-Tabary, COMMENTARY ON THE QUR'AN. (Tafser) dar Al-Kotob-Al-Ilmiyah, Beirut, Lebanon (1999)

How Islam Plans to change the world, by William WAGNER. Published by Kregel publications, a division of Kregel, Inc. 2004

Ibn Hisham, Al-Sira Al-Nabawi .Dar Ibn Hazm publication, Beirut, Lebanon

Ibn Ishaq, Sirat Rasul Allah, The life of Muhammad, Trns. A. Guillaume (New York: Oxsford University Press, 1980)

Islam the straight path, John L. Esposito, New York Oxford, Oxford University press 2005

Jalalan, Al Commentary of Al Jalalan (1983)

Josephus, Flavius. The complete Works of Josephus,. Translated by Wihitson, Kregel Publications, Grand Rapids, MI (1981)

Islam Revealed, by Anis Shorrosh, ( Nashville: Thomas Nelson,1988)

Islam Invasion Confronting the world's faster religion, Robert Morey, Published by Harvest House Publishers, 1992

Light Force, A Stirring Account of the church Caught in the Middle East Crossfire, by Brother Andrew and Al Janssen, published Fleming H. Revell a division of Baker publishing Group, 2004

Muhammad the prophet of Allah. Translated by Dr. Abdel Halim Muhamoud Published by Dar Al Maaraf Cairo, Egypt, (1119)

M.H. Haykal, Life of Muhammad (Plainfield, Ind.: American Trust Publication, 1976)

"Prayers for the persecuted church in Sudan,: CBN News, 12 December 1999.

Sahih Al Bukhari Imam Bukhari Abn Abdullah Mohammad Ben Ishmael Al Bukhari (194-256 H)

Secret of the Koran by Don Richardson Published by Regal Books, 2003

Legal opinion, by Sheikh Mohammad Mutwaly Al-Sha'rawi Cairo, Egypt (no date)

Summery of Sahaih Al Bukhari by Muhammad Nasser Al Dean Al Albany (981-1401)

Tafsir Abn Katheir By Muhammad Ali Al Sabony. Published by Dar Al Qur'an Beirute (1302-1981 AD) 1-3 Volumes

The Book of Hadith Sayings of the prophet Muhammad, from the Mishkat al-Masabih selected by Charles Le Gai Eaton. Re-translated by Mohamoud Mostafa edited by Kabir Helminski & Jeremy Henzell-Thomas . First book Foundation edition published (2008)

The Legucy of Jihad: Islamic Holy War and the Fate of Non-Muslims Edited by Andrew G. Bostom, MD. Forward by Ibn Warraq Published by Prometheus Book (2008)

The Qur'an and the Bible in the light of history and science Dr. William F. Campbell M.D. second edition by Arab World Ministry (2002)

The Wives of the Prophet by Muhammad Saleh Awad Published by The chosen company (2001)

The Opinions (Al Fatawy) 1-10, Mohammad Mutwaly Al Sha'rawi Cairo, Egypt, (No date)

The wives of Rasuol Allah, by Muhammad Salah Awad, Published by the choosen company , Cairo, Egypt (2001)

The Search for the Messiah, Mark Eastman, Chuck smith Forward by Chuck Missler, published by Joy publishing —revised and expanded edition 1996

The Unseen face of Islam, by Bill Musk (London: Monarch, 1989)

'The Muslim mind, by Charles Waddy. (London: Longman, 1976)

Tahzeb Seirt Ibn Hisham. By Abdul Salam Haroun. Published by Al Magmaa Al-Alami Al-Arabi. (No date)

Three Cups of Tea, One man's Mission to promote Peace. One school at a time, Greg Mortenson and David Oliver Relin, First Published by Viking Penguin, 2006

Why I am not a Muslim by Ibn Warraqa, Published by Prometheus Book, 2003

Why we left Islam Former Muslims Speaks out, Stories Compiled and Edited by Susan Crimp & Joel Richardson, Published by Wnd Books, Inc 2008

You Ask and Islam Answers - Al Sharawy, Dar Al Muslim, 1982

Mushaf Al Masinah An-nabawiyah, ed., The Holy Quran (Saudi Arabia: king fahad printing Complex, 1956

Women of Paradise (1) Muhammad Ali Abul Alabbas, 1987, Qur'an's Library

# References

1. Flavius Josephus Book 19, section 3
2. History of Tabary, part 3, Hadith 176, Sahih Muslim, part 2 page 1442
3. The Successors Of The Prophet, page 93
4. Sunan El Nasai Hadith 3148
5. Al Nassai/Bab Neekh/ hadith 3148
6. Mohammed the prophet of Allah by Dr. Abdel Halim Mahmoud 322
7. Abdel Halmin Mahmoud, pg.87
8. Bukhari: 379
9. Sinn el Nisae Hadith 3148
10. Mohammed the prophet of Allah by Dr. Abdel Halim Mahmoud 322
11. Shih Bukhary Volume 4, Book 55, Number 641
12. Bukhary Volume 8, Hadith 319
13. Bukhary Volume 12 Hadith 4548

14. Sahih Bukhari 6:71
15. Ibn Kathir, page 535
16. Ibn Kathir, page 523
17. Sahih Al-Bukhari part 6 page 2561
18. Encyclopedia of Religion, ed. Gibb 1:406
19. Encyclopedia of Religion, eds. Paul Meagher 1:117
20. Bukhari Part 2, Page 183
21. Tabary page 17 page 187
22. Jalalan page 282
23. Ibn Hisham's, The Prophetic Biography, part 2, page 126
24. Ibn Warqa page 34-36
25. Legal opinion  page 36
26. Mohammed the prophet of Allah by Dr. Abdel Halim Mhamoud page 322
27. Mosnad Ahamed ben Hambel part 4 page 73

# Glossary of
# Arabic & Islamic Terms

**ABU** - FATHER OF

**ABU BAKR** - THE FIRST SUCCESSOR TO THE PROPHET MOHAMMAD

**ADHAAN** - THE CALL TO PRAYER

**AL-HAJAR AL-ASWAD** - THE BLACK STONE

**AL-AZEEM** - THE GREAT

**AHL AL-KITAB** - PEOPLE OF THE BOOK - BOTH JEWS AND CHRISTIANS

**AL-HAWARIYUN** - THE DISCIPLES OF JESUS

**AL-MASSIEH** - MESSIAH

**AISHA** - MUHAMMAD'S SECOND WIFE (BETROTHED AT SEVEN YEARS OF AGE) AND THE DAUGHTER OF ABU BAKR

**ALI** - SON-IN-LAW AND COUSIN OF THE PROPHET MOHAMMAD. CONSIDERED THE FOURTH CALIPH OF SUNNI ISLAM AND THE FIRST CALIPH OF SHIA ISLAM

**ALLAH** - THE GOD OF ISLAM

**ALLAH AKBAR** - GOD IS GREAT

**ALLAHUMMA** - MY LORD

**AL-NASIKH** - WE

**AL-MANSUKH** - THIS REFERS TO THE VERSES IN THE QUR'AN THAT HAVE BEEN ABROGATED AND REPLACED.

**AL-AZEEM** - THE GREAT

**ASSALAMU ALAIKUM** - A GREETING MEANING "PEACE BE UPON YOU"

**AZAR** - A DRESS

**BOHIRA** - A NESTORIAN MONK WHO BLESSED YOUNG MUHAMMAD, PREDICTING THAT HE WOULD BECOME A GREAT PROPHET

**CALIPH** - TITLE OF SUCCESSIVE ISLAMIC LEADERS AFTER MUHAMMAD'S DEATH

**EL HAMMDAH** - THANKSGIVING TO GOD

**EL NEEMA** - THE GRACE OF GOD

**EID-UL-FITR** - THE FEAST WHICH FOLLOWS THE LAST DAY OF RAMADAN

**EID-UL-ADHA** - THE FEAST OF THE "MOMENTOUS SACRIFICE" COMMEMORATING ABRAHAM'S WILLINGNESS TO SACRIFICE HIS SON.

**EID MUBARAK** - WISHING YOU A BLESSED CELEBRATION

**IN SHA' ALLAH** - GOD WILLING

**GOHANAM** - HELL

**HABIBI** - TERM OF AFFECTION MEANING "BELOVED"

**HADITH** - A SAYING OR TEACHING OF MUHAMMAD

**HAG** - TITLE GIVEN TO A PERSON WHO HAS FULFILLED THE PILGRIMAGE TO MECCA

**HAGZ** - UNDERGROUND ROOM

**HAJJ** - PILGRIMAGE TO MECCA AND ONE OF THE FIVE PILLARS OF ISLAM

**HALAL** - ALLOWED (AS OPPOSED TO BEING FORBIDDEN)

**HARAM** - FORBIDDEN

**HEGAAB** - THE VEIL

**HIJRA** - MUHAMMAD'S MIGRATION FROM MECCA TO MEDINA IN AD 622. THE STARTING OF THE MUSLIM RELIGIOUS CALENDAR, MARKING THE INCEPTION OF ISLAM

**HWAA'** - EVE

**HOURI** - ONE OF THE BEAUTIFUL VIRGINS OF THE QUR'ANIC PARADISE

**IBLIS** - SATAN

**IBN OR BIN** - SON OF

**IBN ALLAH** - SON OF GOD

**IBRAHIM** - ABRAHAM

**IFTAR** - THE MEAL THAT BREAKS THE FAST OF RAMADAN

**IMAM** - THE MUSLIM SPIRITUAL LEADER OF A LOCAL MOSQUE

**INJIL** - THE ARABIC WORD FOR THE NEW TESTAMENT OR GOSPEL

**ISSA (OR ISA)** - JESUS

**ISHMAEL** - THE SON OF ABRAHAM THROUGH HAGAR

**ISLAM** - THE RELIGION OF THE MUSLIMS FOUNDED BY THE PROPHET MUHAMMAD. LITERALLY - SUBMISSION TO THE WILL OF ALLAH

**JAHILIYYA** - ACCORDING TO ISLAM - THE AGE OF PRE-ISLAMIC TRIBALISM OR - THE DAYS OF IGNORANCE CHARACTERIZED BY PAGAN PRACTICES.

**JANNATU** - THE GARDEN OF EDEN BEFORE ADAM AND EVE SINNED. ALSO, THE PARADISE OR HEAVEN OF ISLAM

**JIHAD** - HOLY WAR

**JINN** - SPIRITUAL BEINGS OR DEMONS

**JIZYA** - A TAX IMPOSED ON NON-MUSLIMS LIVING IN ISLAMIC LANDS

**KA'ABA** - HOUSE OF ALLAH, A SQUARE BUILDING IN MECCA CONTAINING THE BLACK ROCK. MUSLIMS BELIEVE THAT ABRAHAM AND ISHMAEL BUILT THIS SITE AS A HOUSE OF PRAYER

**KA'AK** - SWEET COOKIES MUSLIMS EAT FOR EID-UL-FITR

**KAFIR** - INFIDEL

**KALIMATUHUU** - A TERM MEANING "THE WORD OF GOD." ALSO USED AS A REFERENCE TO ISSA (JESUS) IN THE QUR'AN

**KETAB** - A BOOK

**KHADIJA** - MUHAMMAD'S FIRST WIFE, A WEALTHY WOMAN FROM THE TRIBE OF QURAYSH AND 15 YEARS MUHAMMAD'S SENIOR.

**KHOBTH** - BREAD

**KULLU AM WA ANTUM** - EVERY YEAR YOU...

**BI-KHAIR** - MAY YOU BE WELL THROUGH THE YEAR

**LA ALLAH ALA ALLAH** - THERE IS NO OTHER GOD BUT ALLAH

**LABBAIK** - ANSWERING GOD'S CALL

**LAHM** - MEAT

**LAILATUL-QADR** - THE 27TH NIGHT OF RAMADAN - MOST HOLY NIGHT. ALSO REFERRED TO AS THE NIGHT THAT IS "BETTER THAN A THOUSAND MONTHS."

**LA SHARIKA LK** - CONFESSION WHICH MEANS, "NO OTHER PARTNERS WITH ALLAH"

**LAILAT AL-QADER** - THE TWENTY-SEVENTH NIGHT OF RAMADAN. THE NIGHT MOHAMMAD RECEIVED HIS FIRST "REVELATION". MUSLIM'S BELIEVE THAT THIS IS THE DAY HEAVEN OPENS AND THAT ALLAH GRANTS THEIR PRAYERS

**MAHDI** - A COMING WORLD LEADER IN ISLAMIC ESCHATOLOGY

**MADRASSAH** - AN ISLAMIC RELIGIOUS SCHOOL

**MAWLID AL-NABI** - CELEBRATION OF THE BIRTHDAY OF MUHAMMAD

**MECCA (OR MEKKA)** - ISLAM'S MOST HOLY CITY. THE CITY OF MUHAMMAD'S BIRTH

**MEDINA (OR MADINA)** - ISLAM'S SECOND MOST HOLY CITY. THE CITY MOHAMMAD FLED TO IN AD 622

**MARIAM** - MARY, THE MOTHER OF JESUS

**MUTAWAFICA** - TERM MEANING -TO CAUSE TO DIE. USED OF ALLAH IN REFERRING TO THE DEATH OF JESUS IN SURAH 3:55

**MOSQUE** - A MUSLIM PLACE OF WORSHIP

**MOWAD** - DIVINE APPOINTMENT

**MUEZZIN** - THE MUSLIM CLERIC WHO ANNOUNCES THE FIVE DAILY CALLS TO PRAYER

**MUHAMMAD (OR MOHAMMAD)** - THE PROPHET OF ISLAM. ALLAH'S FINAL AND GREATEST PROPHET. OTHER NAMES IN THE QUR'AN AND HADITHS REFERRING TO MUHAMMAD ARE AHMED, MOSTAFA AND MAHMMOUD

**MUJAHIDEN** - MUSLIMS WHO FIGHT FOR ALLAH AND ISLAM

**MUSLIM** - A FOLLOWER OF ISLAM

**NIKAAH** - MARRIAGE OR SEXUAL INTERCOURSE

**PBUH** - PEACE BE UPON HIM. USED AS A TERM OF REVERENCE WHEN UTTERING THE NAME OF MUHAMMAD

**QATELOW** - DECREE MEANING, "KILL THEM"

**QUR'AN** - THE HOLY BOOK OF ISLAM. CONSIDERED TO BE THE WORDS OF ALLAH GIVEN TO THE PROPHET MUHAMMAD. THE LITERAL MEANING IS "RECITATION"

**QAHOWA** - COFFEE

**RAMADAN** - THE NINTH MONTH OF THE LUNAR CALENDAR, SUPPOSEDLY WHEN THE ANGEL GABRIEL GAVE MUHAMMAD HIS FIRST REVELATION

**RASSOUL OR NABI** - GOD'S MESSENGER - A COLLECTIVE TERM FOR THE PROPHETS

**RUHUN MINHU** - THE SPIRIT FROM GOD

**SAIF** - SWORD

**SALEEB** - CROSS

**SALAM** - CUSTOMARY ARABIC GREETING MEANING - PEACE

**SALAT** - THE FIVE DAILY PRAYERS PRESCRIBED IN ISLAM

**SAWM** - THE FAST HOURS DURING RAMADAN

**SHAHDA** - THE CREED OF ISLAM MEANING "THERE IS ONLY ONE GOD, ALLAH, AND MUHAMMAD IS HIS PROPHET"

**SHAI** - TEA

**SHARIA** - THE ENTIRE BODY OF ISLAMIC LAW AND JURISPRUDENCE

**SHI'ITE** - A FOLLOWER OF SHIA ISLAM, THE BRANCH OF ISLAM WITH THE SECOND LARGEST FOLLOWING. LITERALLY - THE FOLLOWERS OF ALI

**SHIRK** - IDOLATRY OR BLASPHEMY AGAINST ALLAH. BELIEVING IN OTHER GODS BESIDE ALLAH

**SUNNAH** - THE WRITTEN TRADITIONS OF THE PROPHET MUHAMMAD AS CONTAINED IN THE HADITH

**SUNNI** - THE BRANCH OF ISLAM ADHERED TO BY MOST MUSLIMS. FOLLOWERS OF MUHAMMAD'S SUCCESSORS ABU BAKR, AND UMAR. LITERALLY, "PEOPLE OF THE WAY"

**SURAH/SURA** - CHAPTER IN THE QUR'AN

**SUHOOR** - THE MEAL MUSLIMS EAT BEFORE SUNRISE DURING RAMADAN

**TAFSIR** - A COMMENTARY ON THE QUR'AN

**TAHRIF** - THE TEACHING THAT DEEMS THE BIBLE A CORRUPTED BOOK.

**TAQIYA** - DISSIMULATION OR DECEPTION FOR THE CAUSE OF ALLAH AND THE ADVANCEMENT OF ISLAM. CONCEALING OR DISGUISING ONE'S BELIEFS, CONVICTIONS, OR STRATEGIES DURING WAR OR AT A TIME OF IMMINENT DANGER

**TAQIYYA** - JIHAD

**TARIQ** - A MESSENGER OR ONE WHO LEADS THE WAY.

**TAWHID** - NO OTHER GOD BUT ALLAH - EMPHASIZING THE ONENESS OF GOD.

**TAWAF** - THE ACT OF WALKING IN ROTATION AROUND THE KA'BA IN MECCA,

PERFORMED AS PART OF THE HAJJ

**TAYAMMUM** - RUBBING HANDS AND FEET WITH SAND INSTEAD OF WATER PERFORMING WUDU WHEN NO WATER CAN BE FOUND, SUCH AS IN A DESERT ENVIRONMENT

**UMAR (OMAR)** - THE SECOND SUCCESSOR TO MUHAMMAD

**UMMA** - MUSLIM COMMUNITY OR FELLOWSHIP

**WARAQA IBN NOFAL** - THE COUSIN OF KHADIGA (MUHAMMAD'S FIRST WIFE) WHO WAS A JEWISH CONVERT TO CHRISTIANITY AND THEN LATER TO ISLAM

**WE** - IN THE QUR'AN, THE FIRST PERSON PLURAL IN REFERENCE TO ALLAH

**WUDU** - RITUAL WASHING WITH WATER (ABLUTIONS) BEFORE PRAYER

**YAWM** - A DAY

**YAWM AL GOMAA** - FRIDAY

**YAWM AL-DIN** - THE DAY OF JUDGMENT

**YAWM AL-QIYAMAH** - THE DAY OF RESURRECTION

**ZABUR** - THE BOOK OF PSALMS BY DAVID (ZABUR OF DAWOOD)

**ZAKAT** - MANDATORY GIVING. IT IS REQUIRED THAT EVERY MUSLIM GIVE ONE-FOURTH OF HIS OR HER INCOME TO THE MOSQUE

**ZAYNAB BINT JAHSH** - ONE OF MUHAMMAD'S WIVES. ORIGINALLY ZAYNAB WAS MUHAMMAD'S DAUGHTER-IN-LAW THROUGH HIS ADOPTED SON. UPON COMMAND OF ALLAH, MUHAMMAD TOOK HER FOR HIS WIFE BY HAVING HIS ADOPTED SON DIVORCE HER

**ZAWAG** - MARRIAGE

**ZAWAJ AL MUT'AA** - THE PRACTICE OF TEMPORARY MARRIAGE OR "PLEASURE MARRIAGE"